BETTER THAN THEM

BETTER THAN THEM

The Unmaking of an Alabama Racist

S. McEachin Otts

Foreword by Frye Gaillard

NewSouth Books

Montgomery

NewSouth Books
105 S. Court Street
Montgomery, AL 36104

Publisher's Cataloging-in-Publication data

Otts, S. McEachin
Better than them : the unmaking of an Alabama racist
/ S. McEachin Otts

p. cm.

ISBN: 978-1-60306-343-2 (pbk)
ISBN: 978-1-60306-344-9 (ebook)

I. Title.

2014952961

Printed in the United States of America

To the citizens of my hometown who seek harmony and progress, and to people everywhere who dared protest nonviolently for the right to vote—for themselves, those they loved, and coming generations.

Racism: a belief that race is the primary determinant of human traits and capacities and that racial differences produce an inherent superiority of a particular race.

— MERRIAM-WEBSTER DICTIONARY

CONTENTS

Eight pages of photographs follow page 76.

FOREWORD

FRYE GAILLARD

In the summer of 1965, the civil rights movement came to Greensboro, Alabama, and Mac Otts was there to greet it with a tire iron. In this candid and heartfelt memoir, he recounts his own transformation from small-town racist in the Alabama Black Belt through the realms of remorse to an understanding of our shared history rooted in fundamental good will. There's value in the honesty of his account, but more than that, there is an impressive breadth of perspective at the heart of the story.

When most of us think of the civil rights years, we remember the most iconic moments—Rosa Parks refusing to relinquish her seat on the bus, Martin Luther King Jr. proclaiming his dream at the March on Washington, the terrible bombing of a Birmingham church that killed four beautiful and innocent girls. These were, in fact, the defining moments in a movement that touched the heart and captured the imagination of America. But as Otts reminds us, the movement was more than a national crusade. It was also intensely local, a struggle that came to virtually every community in the South, and many in other areas as well.

Sometimes these small-town struggles, these less-heralded demands for simple justice, were the most intense and heroic of all. When, for example, King came to Greensboro to add his voice to those of the indigenous leaders, the Ku Klux Klan set out to kill him. That was the word on the streets at least, and a Greensboro foot soldier named Theresa Burroughs risked her own life to save Dr. King's, giving him shelter until the marauding Klansmen had called off their search.

Such moments form the heart of civil rights history—these numberless, extraordinary acts of courage performed by people with names now forgotten.

In the pages of *Better Than Them*, these examples come alive once again—a representative sampling of them, at least—against the steamy backdrop of a small Southern town. But there is more to the story than that. Otts reminds us as well that the civil rights movement affected us all, raising the most basic questions about who we were and what we believed and what kind of place we wanted ours to be.

Most of us claimed to believe in democracy, in the notion of equality in the eyes of the law. But before the transformations of the civil rights years, we seldom lived our lives that way. Nor did we honor our articles of faith, most often learned in Sunday school, that we were all children of God and therefore brothers and sisters of one another. The civil rights movement forced us to confront these dismal hypocrisies—these desperate notions that we were "better than them"—and if we allowed our hearts and minds to respond, it made us all a little more free.

In the telling of his own story, Mac Otts brings new life to this under-standing, this liberating truth given to us all by a hard and heroic moment in history. The story may begin with ugly revelations of ignorance and fear, but it also affirms the possibility of change. In our current time of national gridlock and division, we need these reminders, I think, that things can get better . . . in our own lives and in the life of the country in which we live.

FRYE GAILLARD *is writer-in-residence at the University of South Alabama and the author of more than twenty books on Southern history, politics, and culture.*

PREFACE

The racist experience is often buried deep within people like me—people who changed. I remain amazed at the grip racism had on my mind and heart in 1965, and what it compelled me to do. I also am amazed at the different person I have become. This book represents my best attempt to understand what happened to me and the cultures in which I lived as a nurtured racist. I hope it plants a seed for new reflection and communication, for a fresh and open dialogue on race relations—one that contrasts with often-dominating political correctness and typical approaches to the topic.

My initial motivations were entirely personal with no thought of publication. My wife and I adopted a wonderful son of mixed race, and that made the personal even more personal. I saw how some people responded to us as a mixed family. It forced the question of my own attitude from years before to a higher level, and I wanted to understand even more about the powerful grip that racism had on me and so many others. What made me the racist I was then? And equally important, what caused me to change? What about the cultures, institutions, and individuals that nurtured my perspectives? What empowered them, and have they changed?

While the questions were the same, I gained a new motivation toward publication from my students in college classes who gave me the idea that there is a pressing need for this type of real-world dialogue on relations between the races.

ACKNOWLEDGMENTS

My wife's loving support and common sense in this rigorous journey was indispensable. Our daughter and son inspired me, and their children provided needed distractions! My dear sister and brother-in-law plus a treasured mix of nephews and nieces, have supported bold wanderings through our wonderful and awful family history. My nephew, Dr. David Nelson, helped in versatile ways.

Frye Gaillard, Author in Residence for the University of South Alabama, provided ongoing consultation that made a big difference. D. Fran Morley was a creative and diligent editing cohort, and my NewSouth editor, Randall Williams, provided diligence and experience. A creative photographer, Zach Riggins, brought much to life. Anne Sledge Bailey was helpful beyond her interview, and all interviewed were so responsive and open. Members of my sociology classes at Faulkner University, Mobile branch, helped me catch a greater vision. Perseverance to completion came purely by God's grace!

BETTER THAN THEM

I

BLACK BELT HEAT: THE MARCH

I had been an eighteen-year-old racist in 1965 when I stood with other whites in my hometown of Greensboro, Alabama, gripping a tire iron in defiant opposition to a lawful and peaceful civil rights march.

Now, forty summers afterward, I was back in Greensboro. On a sunny Sunday afternoon, my wife and I drove into town, and I parked our car outside an office building on the lot where the Gulf gas station once stood. Of course, no one was around. It was as hot as it had been on the day of the march. We stood on the curb and looked across the street at the stone Confederate sentinel statue and the Hale County Courthouse looming behind and above it. I took a few photos of the statue and courthouse. It all looked much the same, except smaller than remembered. To that date, I had never attended a class reunion after high school. Positive memories—and I did have many—were accompanied by heavy, dark shadows. I surfaced as the proverbial prodigal while researching this book, due to associated contacts with good people.

My wife stepped toward the street. I held back, telling her I wanted to take a few more pictures, but actually I wanted the pain to subside. After a few minutes, we crossed over to the sentinel on its pedestal, and while its expression was as straightforward, stoic, and resolute as ever, the years had taken their toll. The stone figure was scarred and chipped—not unlike me.

On returning to the site that summer day, I was overwhelmed by searing memories of what had been inside me and had controlled me in 1965. It's difficult to give such emotions adequate burials. For me, it took forty years and facing the sentinel to complete the process, and still the shadows lingered.

On the drive home, I wondered how others were affected by the day of that march. It was not a central moment in the civil rights movement, and it received scant media mention. I can say only that it was significant for me.

1965

The dripping humidity was quite normal in Alabama's Black Belt on Friday, July 16, 1965. With temperatures well into the nineties, it felt even hotter down in the service well at the Gulf station where I stood beneath a car—as hot as Hades, to use one of the more polite expressions of the day. Regardless of the heat, it was an apt description of the service well where I drained the oil from cars and pickups and used an air gun to shoot grease into their steering and suspension joints. I was sweating at my uncle's service station to earn spending money for the fall and my first year at college.

My parents were rich in nothing but family tradition, but that tradition and Greensboro town culture made it convenient and even acceptable for my father to pretend that he still had our ancestors' wealth in his own pockets. Pretense was not necessarily sin in my hometown. Some was integral.

Along with her rough eccentricities and soft side, my grandmother, Jack—it was her chosen nickname—carried family pride like a big scroll, ready to roll out the ancestral listings at the slightest opportunity. She liked to sit in her big chair and proudly speak to me of our Scottish Robert-the-Bruce lineage and whatever else pleased her. One day, Jack called me close to her chair and whispered: *You are better than them. Don't forget it.*

My reply consisted of something profound like *Okay.* Notwithstanding the usual fond front-door greetings from her so-called servants and the laughs I shared with the one bringing us refreshments, I had no doubt what Jack meant: *You are white. You are better than any black. You have privilege because you were born white and they were not.* Concise and heavy, her "better than them" words composed the first formal edict for racism in my life. Jack died in my adolescence, but her words endured for a young, impressionable boy who wanted so badly to see himself as special.

Considering the kind treatment received that day and every day from the black women employed in Jack's household, I did not need more explanation to know the relative context for her pronouncement. There was much more to come in the construction of this racist, but Jack's pronouncement was a formal start as far as my memory goes.

I was eighteen that sweltering day at the service station. My daydreams were at least some distraction from the heat; I was looking forward to driving forty miles north with my parents to the University of Alabama in about six weeks for fall enrollment. But until my breakaway, I was stuck with the humdrum of Greensboro, the town of three thousand people where I was born and raised. That's how I saw that Friday: just another humdrum day in a humdrum town. I had no idea that the day was about to take a turn that would form an unforgettable mark in time, one that defied dreams of glories past and future. I was about to come face-to-face with white Greensboro's nightmare.

After removing the car's drain plug to let its engine oil flow through a funnel into a big barrel, I climbed out from the well and walked forward into stunning sunlight just outside the raised garage door, drawing long, deep breaths of fresh air. I looked directly across the two-lane Main Street that ran east and west in front of the Hale County Courthouse. The courthouse and the service station marked the beginning of a small downtown area that stretched to my right down Main Street for four or five blocks. The scene across the street was the same as always in summer: rippling waves of heat danced on scorched asphalt.

My usual flights of fantasy—of courtroom theatrics or sentinel heroism—didn't begin that day; instead, I cocked my head, trying to make out a strange sound coming from somewhere down Main Street. It was a constant mumbling with occasional escalations of volume. It sounded like nothing I had heard before. Across the street, a few shirt-and-tie men, court and county officials, scurried out through the oversized wooden front doors of the courthouse and stopped on the porch, at the top of a short flight of stone steps. They leaned forward, ties dangling, obviously listening to the same sound that had caught my attention. The men could not have heard the sound from inside the courthouse with window air conditioners droning. They must have been told about it.

The noise was increasing in volume and I recognized it as a cacophony of human voices. I made my way out to the curb with my uncle and a co-worker. We were totally mesmerized and didn't speak to each other. We watched the group on the courthouse porch; a couple of sheriff's deputies in brown uniforms and hats, one carrying a rifle by his side, had now joined the others. They went out into Main Street, looking directly toward a growing crowd of people on the sidewalk to their left—white men yelling in loud, raucous voices that were not clear enough for me to understand.

I and others on our side stepped into the street, and deputies came across to tell us to back off and stay on the curb. Soon, the front few lines of black marchers emerged in the street, having been obscured by a corner building. As the now-obvious civil rights demonstration advanced, I was shocked to see a few white marchers in their midst.

Four months earlier, March 7, 1965—Bloody Sunday, as it came to be called—marked a pivotal point of organized marches in Alabama when demonstrators were beaten by state and local lawmen at the Edmund Pettus Bridge in Selma. The marchers were on their way to Montgomery to present grievances to Governor George C. Wallace. The state-sanctioned violence of that day sent shock waves across America.

I had seen the TV reports of Bloody Sunday, but never thought it or any other demonstrations that summer would affect me or Greensboro in the long run. Surely our community was more insulated, and such "irritations" would pass. My father was a former deputy and still one of the "good old boys" trusted by authorities. I was not alone in my belief that he and others like him would not allow such nonsense as civil rights to affect our established way of life. Now, watching a group of blacks and whites march toward the courthouse in Greensboro, I was outrageously offended. I was sure the local blacks were being stirred into a rebellious state of mind, mostly by outsiders who hated us. To me at that time, unsubmissive blacks were totally unacceptable in our society.

Across the street on the corner, a few local white men held crude weapons—pipes or sticks likely picked up nearby. Something hot inside me made me run back to the station and pick up a tire iron. It was about eighteen inches long and heavy in my hands.

I ran back to the curbside where the crowd had swelled, nudged my way into place, and held the tire iron by my side opposite the deputy twenty feet away. He probably would have told me to put my weapon down if he had noticed, but like everyone else, he was totally focused on the approaching marchers. In my recollection today, I had no purposeful thought; emotion dominated, and anger was at the boiling point. These marchers dared to block public streets and challenge our symbols of authority to express their rebellious, evil intentions! They wanted to steal my dreams and my pride, to turn the tables on white people. They had been brainwashed into thinking *they* were better than *us*!

It occurred to me that someone might die a violent death that day. My foregone conclusion was that it would be a black or white demonstrator. I was too young to see myself as vulnerable. I don't know if the term *good riddance* passed through my mind, but it was certainly possible. I had no sympathy for anyone being attacked in the demonstrations I saw on television. They deserved it. Iron in my hands and my heart, I did not think that this was history in the making. Those marchers dared to challenge my values, heritage, and pride: there was no alternative view for me at the time; I just did not have it in me. While black advocates spoke out on television from places like Montgomery and Birmingham, not one local black person or any protagonist had ever broached the subject of black voting rights— or any other black rights—with me. I had never heard anyone on a local level, black or white, speak publicly in support of equal rights. Sure, I had a limited awareness of demonstrations in Selma and other places, but that awareness carried no weight with me in those days. I preferred my dreams over nightmares. I needed my dreams.

Suddenly, the silence was broken by blaring sirens as two highway patrol cars pulled up to block the intersection of Main and Centreville streets— creating a barrier to traffic and marchers on the east courthouse corner. Uniformed officers got out and assumed positions on the courthouse steps where several other patrolmen, a handful of deputies, the sheriff, and a few town policemen had already posted themselves. The mayor and a few town officials were standing on the porch. One policeman was slowly patting a billy club in the palm of his hand, just as I had begun to do with my tire iron. All eyes, like mine, were going back and forth from the courthouse porch to the rowdy group of onlookers, some openly wielding weapons, then to the marchers who were closing in and about to step between us and the courthouse.

A few officers blocked the sidewalk across Main at a side street that ran down the west side of the courthouse. The rowdy crowd of white Greensboro men increased and massed at that corner as demonstrators came nearer. They were shouting and jeering: *Go back to Africa, niggers! You dumb nigger! Your black ass is in trouble now!* And to the occasional white marcher, *Nigger lover!* Those of us in the lesser crowd in front of the gas station were mostly mute—maybe dumbfounded. Many of those shouting on the opposite corner had probably worked themselves into a mob-like frenzy while following the march up Main.

The hatred and tension were palpable. Tightening my grip on the tire iron, I held it to my side. In the other crowd, more men were brandishing hoses and pipes or sticks. I felt reinforced and emboldened—without a logical plan of action—filled with mute anger and a high-key readiness to react. It was a matter of meeting the stinging reality of a civil rights movement that even Greensboro could not avoid: a force that all of my family and community history and traditions stood against. The collision was inevitable.

In time, for me, the conflict would not remain external.

Approaching the courtyard corner, the lead marchers slowed and stopped completely as others stacked up behind them. In the center, a formally dressed black man—seemingly a minister—held a black Bible with both hands. From the look on his face, he held his tool as tightly as I did mine. His lead row began slowly walking again, turned right onto the sidewalk bordering Main Street and the courtyard, and then stopped. Others moved beside, around, and behind them to fill up Main Street and the sidewalk, facing the sentinel and courthouse. All were completely silent. We faced their backs, some only four or five feet from us. None of them looked back—astounding!

White spectators filled in around our position in front of the station while the heckling core remained on the corner opposite, now to the right front of the demonstrators. At first, a few officers kept a growing number of hecklers on the other side limited to the sidewalk area of Main Street, but they must have eventually left their position or allowed the crowd to spill over into a small street bordering that side of the courtyard. From our slightly elevated position, we could look between or over the heads of the marchers to view the steps where several officers still stood. A few held rifles, muzzles down; others had holstered handguns and billy clubs in hand.

There must have been at least a hundred demonstrators—younger teenage blacks, older teens, young adult and middle-aged blacks, and several older adults. Most I didn't recognize. Some were locals, although I didn't know them well. A handful of young adult whites were scattered through the group, obviously from out of town. Later, I learned that many were college students from places like UCLA or Princeton. To me, they were traitors to their own race: outsiders thinking they were smarter and better, even so impertinent as to consider themselves made of better stuff than veterans of World Wars! Many of us thought their attitudes nothing short of asinine. I probably hated them even more than black demonstrators, though I knew nothing about them. It did not matter.

The number of highway patrolmen, deputies, and policemen quickly multiplied on the porch steps and front sides of the courtyard. Marchers filled the yard and spilled out onto Main Street. Those at the front stopped short of the first courthouse step. Though not described in news accounts, there was a significant pause in the midst of all the activity and noise. Protestors stood virtually soundless, even the heckling subsided. There was some shifting among the demonstrators. Then, all movement ceased completely, and one lone female voice began singing "Amazing Grace." Other marchers joined the chorus. It was a quiet, heartfelt version of the hymn: *Amazing Grace, how sweet the sound that saved a wretch like me. I once was lost, but now I'm found; was blind but now I see.* It was only a few verses followed by momentary silence—the kind when seconds are more like minutes.

In front of the Gulf station, I stood holding the tire iron, transfixed by the scene. Suddenly, the big courthouse clock gonged on the hour, and the old familiar sound startled me. The clock's tones, so clear in that moment of silence, rang out more than once—as if on cue, synchronized with the crisis.

Hymn or not, heckling renewed with even more volume. A car that had been in our shop was parked with its front bumper close to the Gulf sign near where I was standing, and I stepped up onto the car's front bumper, leaning with my free hand against the thick metal sign pole. I still held tight to the tire iron, my arm slightly cocked in a ready position, adrenaline pushing me toward whatever came next.

Suddenly there was a scuffle at the foot of the courthouse steps. Pandemonium followed. Officers on the steps ran into the scattering crowd with weapons drawn, pushing the crowd back. Some demonstrators tried to flee, a few stumbling and falling. Some of the white hecklers rushed into the crowd with raised fists or crude weapons. A black woman fell and was helped up by another demonstrator. Around the statue, white men were clubbing and relentlessly pummeling victims with their fists. Shrill screams rose from those victims and others. I saw a woman hit solidly on the chin. Some demonstrators were quickly held at gunpoint by authorities. To my knowledge, no demonstrator retaliated or fought back, but it all happened so fast. With their batons extended, authorities quickly pushed into the crowd and backed up most demonstrators and white attackers. In the confusion, I could not tell if anyone was arrested.

It was years later that I remembered something that had somehow been blocked from my conscious mind. While many demonstrators scattered, I jumped down from my perch on the car bumper. In the chaos and rush, a few ran close by me, and I drew that tire iron back over my head. In the pit of my stomach, I felt a powerful mix of rage, panic, and fear. It could well have surged into the tire iron, but it did not. At some point, I dropped my hands and the iron. In the aftermath, maybe I was in a state of shock. I do not recall talking about that day in detail until years later away from Greensboro. My racial views hadn't changed that day, but surely it was a radical event in my life that I tried to forget—unsuccessfully, as it turned out.

In the heat of a moment, people can do violent things. I was at the wrong place and time, armed, fueled by generations of hate accelerated by a chaotic crowd. I shudder to think what might have happened if any of those fleeing the scene had even brushed me. Their lives and mine could have changed in an instant.

2

LITTLE WOMAN, MEDIA,
CHURCH FIRES, A WHITE NEGRO

I recognized one face as the front line of marchers approached my location. She stood out because she was a little person—a *midget* to us then—known by some as a woman with attitude. I would often see her Saturdays when everyone was out and milling about on Main Street. When whites occasionally stared, she responded with a glaring frown, even in the midst of laughing exchanges with other blacks. Then, mission accomplished, she would return to her conversations—seemingly unperturbed, secure, and gregarious. I never heard anything about her hurting anyone or breaking the law, and whites seemed to tolerate her responses because they viewed her as a harmless curiosity. This allowed teenagers to provoke and return her glare as a type of game.

Continuing to march, the little woman turned her head, and looked directly at me for only a few seconds. It was not the old frowning, aggressive stare, but a very serious look. The games were over. Though I recognized some of the marchers, I did not know any names, not even hers. I knew many black people in town, but few by name. Maybe it was not the same for all white youths growing up in Greensboro, but it was the case for me—as if I could not recognize their humanity with names. I was later to learn more about the daring little woman.

In my hometown, most whites were thoroughly grounded in the culture that nurtured my views—socialized to the core with little or no doubt about the relative positions of blacks and whites. The little woman was simply a *nigger.* My experience growing up had taught me that the term was totally disrespectful—but whites considered it appropriate due to blacks' low status, not subject to challenge.

11

In white conversation, I used only that epithet, now euphemistically said as *the N word*, though I said *colored* at times around black people—my submerged conscience speaking. I was also suspicious of any white person who used *Negro* very much in white conversation; that would mark them as potentially a left-wing radical, not to be trusted. Blacks who participated in demonstrations were considered lower than those who didn't: any blacks trying to assert their rights were objects of white scorn.

As a boy, my relationships with black children were slim to nonexistent. Our worlds were totally separate—where would we get to know each other? Schools and churches were completely segregated. The Strand Theater, managed by my Uncle Scott for a time, was probably the third most likely place for youths to get acquainted—but not interracially. Black moviegoers were relegated to the balcony with its separate stairs opening through a single door directly to the small sidewalk and street on the side of the building. Whites entered the wide front doors into the spacious lobby and sat downstairs.

Other spots in Greensboro for young people to associate were the swimming pool in summer and the Dairy Bar year round. No black person, young or old, was allowed at the swimming pool. At the Dairy Bar, white children and teens not only consumed a lot of ice cream and fast food, but also just hung out, usually in or on parked cars—much like TV images of *Happy Days* but without curb service. On life's flip side in my hometown, black people's money was good at the Dairy Bar, but they were served at a separate window, generally by a black woman, and they never lingered, but took their purchases to their own hangouts. The serving windows were not marked *black* or *white*. Everyone in town just knew. Any stranger who stepped up to the wrong window would have been promptly redirected. While there were no public restrooms at the Dairy Bar, there were some at the few gas stations in town. At least one had a restroom for black people labeled *colored*. My enterprising uncle got his Gulf station after giving up the theater, and it had two restrooms for men and women labeled as such— understood to be for whites only.

The Black Belt was indeed heart of the Bible Belt, and to my knowledge, all Christian churches were segregated. My own experience was that the white churches generally reinforced racism. In fact, from antebellum times to now, it was and is such a uniquely relevant negative and positive factor that churches merit special consideration relative to racism and harmony—more on that and my related experience later. As an experienced believer years afterward, I was not surprised by seeing more clearly this horrendous fault of churches made up of imperfect human beings—just as I'm not surprised by the wonderful things done in God's name to help others and bring people together. We are not living in heaven yet.

At any rate, primary social institutions in my hometown undoubtedly kept black and white youths from really knowing each other while some groups and individuals powerfully reinforced stereotypes and fears of the unknown. In my effort to understand the perspective many of us held that summer of 1965, I reviewed online and microfilm reproductions of *New York Times* and *Greensboro Watchman* accounts. Perhaps not surprisingly, the reports from those two periodicals on events that summer were generally not consistent with each other or with my memory on some crucial facts. The more concise *Times* article was the earlier report due to being a daily publication (the *Watchman* was and is a weekly).

Pickets in Alabama Attacked By Whites

Greensboro, Ala.—July 16 (AP)—A demonstration by about 75 Negroes was broken up today when white bystanders attacked the crowd with sticks, hammers, and rubber hoses.

The brief melee broke out after the demonstrators had refused Mayor William C. Christian's request that they return to the St. Matthew Methodist Church.

The police, sheriff's deputies, and state troopers were using billy clubs to push the demonstrators from the Hale County Courthouse toward the church when the bystanders attacked. Several Negroes were injured and some officers reportedly were shaken up. The Negroes had been picketing the business district for several hours before they gathered at the courthouse. This was the first racial violence in this west central Alabama town where a voter registration campaign is under way.

A much different *Greensboro Watchman* article ran on July 22. While the

Times did not mention the ages of demonstrators, the *Watchman* pointedly did. "They walked in groups, mostly of four, and virtually all of them were juveniles. Some appeared to be no more than 13 or 14 years of age. . . ."

While I remember the majority of marchers as teens and young adults, I don't think juveniles comprised "virtually all" of the demonstrators. This inconsistency alone does not necessarily indicate reporting bias. However, any presumption of absolute objectivity fades as the *Watchman* article continues.

> They carried the customary "civil rights" placards, crudely lettered for the most part, but added a new note to their crusade by leveling personal and abusive attacks on Mayor William C. Christian and the white people of Greensboro in general. Shortly after 2:30 o'clock, the placard bearers converged on the courthouse and paraded for 20 or 30 minutes, in an endless procession along the northern and western sides of the building. Upwards of 100 were in this march, and during the period, people who had business in the courthouse either waited or slipped into the back-door. The mayor issued a permit for this demonstration, and after the allotted time was up, he appeared on the northern portico of the courthouse and asked that the Negroes disperse pointing out that it was no longer a lawful assembly. Most of the Negroes turned to leave, but a few others waved them back, started cursing at the whites, and defied the mayor's order.

Beyond ascribing negative or immature characteristics to their efforts— "crudely lettered"— the report implies demonstrators were purposefully provoking white bystanders. The term *attacks* could only have referred to words rather than physical violence, yet no words were quoted in the article to qualify the statement. While not close enough to hear everything that was said, I never heard any verbally abusive attacks, nor do I recall hearing anything about such later.

One can sense the impatient criticism inherent in *endless procession*, but the marching did not seem like that to me. Claiming that the march inconvenienced people with business at the courthouse indicates another slant. On the other hand, saying that the demonstrators lingered beyond a set time limit and/or that the mayor requested that they leave is credible, as reported by both articles and consistent with nonviolent resistance.

I never heard any cursing from demonstrators. Considering the terrible remarks thrown at them, it would not be surprising if they replied in kind. However, civil rights demonstrators in the 1960s were taught to avoid displays of aggression as contrary to the tactic of peaceful resistance. In contrast to what was reported about demonstrators, the *Watchman* makes no negative comments or disparaging implications about the "several white bystanders"; despite expected bias from the *Watchman*, it still must have been difficult for the demonstrators to read that omission compared to the article's obvious criticism of them.

> A group of white officers, numbering less than a dozen, started pushing the crowd toward the street. At this point, several white bystanders joined in the fracas, using fists and other weapons—but the Negroes soon disbanded, and went flying back to the St. Matthew A.M.E. Church, which they have been using for headquarters for several weeks. At the church, a few of the Negroes armed themselves with brickbats and bottles, and attempted a rally, but they were soon quieted.
>
> Medical treatment awaited any injured Negroes at the Hale County Hospital, but those who reported injuries elected to go to the Good Samaritan Hospital in Selma. There were 17 making this trip. Fourteen were dismissed without treatment as having only superficial injuries: two more were given first aid treatment for blows on the head. Only one, a Negro girl, remained overnight. She had been hit in the jaw, and she stayed over for dental observation. . . .

The marchers never retaliated. I knew nothing about some arming themselves with brickbats and bottles at St. Matthew church later, but who could have been surprised if they had, considering what they had just experienced? The article continued by recounting related events during the days between the courthouse melee and the *Watchman*'s publication.

> A big Ku Klux Klan rally was held at the Greensboro High athletic field the same night, with speeches by Robert Shelton, Matt Murphy and

Bob Creel. Early Saturday night, the two rural churches were reported as burning. One was on the Bates Mill Road and the other on the Akron Short-Cut road. These fires were being investigated both by state and federal officers. Under threat of an injunction similar to the one now operative in Dallas, Perry and other Black Belt counties, the local Board of Registrars agreed not to employ Insert No. 3, the controversial literacy test, that day. As a result, approximately 120 voter applications were received, but none had been graded at mid-week. . . .

The July 19, 1965, *New York Times* reported, regarding the church burnings, that the St. Mark A.M.E. Church in Greensboro proper, and the Elmwood A.M.E. Zion Church several miles north of town, were both burned to the ground. According to the article, Major Cloud, of the Alabama Highway Patrol, said it had not been determined if the fires were deliberate. The *Times* reported that black leaders believed the burnings were the work of arsonists.

Reverend A. T. Days, one of the area's civil rights leaders, served as a minister for both St. Mark and St. Matthew A.M.E. churches. St. Matthew was used as civil rights headquarters and a meeting place for demonstrations such as the one I witnessed; it was a site that received a lot of press attention.

Since the literacy test for voter registration was dropped, it would seem demonstrations had begun to bear fruit. In fact, an article in the *Times* on July 20, 1965, reported that, thereby, another demonstration was averted. However, according to the *Watchman* article, 120 voter applications were received *but not graded* in the aftermath of dropping the test. Given the delayed grading process and alleged arsonists' burning of churches, it is understandable that those planning civil rights operations might not be so easily placated. They had to be keenly aware that the KKK rally stirred passions and could well have related to church burnings the next day. The rally featured Robert Shelton of Tuscaloosa, then the Grand Dragon of a KKK faction and later the so-called Imperial Wizard of the United Klans of America—the largest and one of the most violent KKK factions in the 1960s. Little did I know then that I would have an intense conversation with Shelton six years later.

The violence of the courthouse march was not something that local and state authorities wanted to be repeated and certainly not before national news media which was now paying attention. Soon, it would become apparent that civil rights leaders were not closing shop. Meanwhile, most white residents of Greensboro depended on a less-than-objective Editor Hamner Cobbs and his *Watchman* along with the ever-active word-of-mouth network for information. Not only were *Watchman* reports slanted, but so was information generated by local whites such as the men who hung out at the barbershop—most with nothing to do but stir rumors. Nobody I knew was reading the *New York Times*, and television news did not cover much of what was happening in Greensboro. Given that lack of other news outlets and opinions, my views and those of others were undoubtedly affected more by what we read in the *Watchman* and heard on the street.

On July 26, a week after the church burnings, some activists who were helping with a voter registration campaign in Eutaw—twenty miles away—came to town to participate in a planned demonstration. Thirty-eight years later, I made contact with one of the whites among them. When I reached him, Richard Stephenson—now retired—was teaching and coordinating secondary math programs in Massachusetts. At age twenty-three in 1965, he was enrolled at the University of Illinois when he and other summer-break students, along with some local blacks from Eutaw, came to participate in a large march that would visit both burned black churches. The march was also to begin at St. Matthew, but this time the police had erected a sawhorse barricade to block the procession from crossing the main street in town.

Stephenson's recollection of the event, provided at my request, was precise and chilling. He wrote that for two days a large crowd of black people and a few white supporters such as himself had gathered to sing "freedom songs" at the barricade.

"The day before the arrests came down, the tone had become quite ominous," he recalled. "The main street side of the barricade was filled with local and state cops, several on horseback, most of them carrying gas masks and clubs. At some point that afternoon, after a seemingly eternal standoff, the cops put on their gas masks and, following unheeded orders for us to disperse, they cut loose with a barrage of tear gas."

Stephenson was at the front of the crowd, next to Reverend Gilmore, a black minister from Greene County, when the gassing began.

"There was really nowhere for us to go because the crowd behind us was so thick. Gilmore turned to the people and began singing *Wade in the water, wade in the water, wade in the water, God's gonna trouble the water.*

"With that, there was a cloudburst and rains poured down from what had been, less than an hour earlier, clear blue skies. This, I swear, is true! If I believed in miracles, I'd say that this was one."

According to Stephenson, the rain neutralized the tear gas, or at least minimized its effects, and the crowd was able to disperse without stampeding, with no one hurt.

Stephenson said Jesse Jackson, of the Southern Christian Leadership Conference, and an entourage from Atlanta joined the Greensboro demonstrators the next day, July 28. "We regrouped at the barricade, but this time the local authorities and state troopers didn't waste their tear gas on us. Sometime in the early afternoon they brought in a bunch of school buses and began loading us onto them. They drove this caravan of buses carrying over three hundred people—about equally split between males and females ranging in age from ten to eighty—to Camp Selma prison. I think the trip was about forty miles."

Stephenson wrote that the demonstrators spent the next three days in cramped quarters at Camp Selma: there were two small rooms of about twenty by forty feet with barred windows; one held 150 men and the other 150 women. "It was quite crowded and we couldn't all sit on the ground at the same time (forget about lying down!), so we slept in shifts. It was pretty damned uncomfortable."

The prisoners went on a hunger strike, Stephenson said, as much to avoid having to use the one toilet in the corner of each room as to make a statement. "After three days we were released, thanks to some kind anonymous people who put up their property to bail us out."

At one point, Stephenson—a white man with a sense of humor and solidarity with his black compatriots in the cause—was interviewed by a deputy.

"I told a deputy who asked me if I was 'a white or a nigger' that I was a Negro. This caused something of a commotion, and I was turned over to Sheriff Jim Clark who took me in a back room and had a semi-friendly chat with me for about a half hour. It was a weird scene, but no one beat on me, for which I was much relieved."

I took this description of Stephenson's personal experience in Selma to be humorously understated. While Stephenson was bold, he certainly had reason for fear, though his age—at the time, he was just five years older than I was—may have given him the insulation of youthful feelings of invincibility.

On the other hand, a few weeks earlier, when I had stood with tire tool in hand, I had little reason for fear. As the son of a former deputy and acquainted with local officers, I had no reason to think Highway Patrolmen were any threat to me.

3

The Spin, the Bubble, and the Vote

As with the courthouse march, there was some spin to the *Watchman* account on July 29, 1965, of events described by Richard Stephenson. This piece was titled, "300 under arrest after they refuse to leave street," and it contended that "Upwards of 90 percent of those arrested were between 16 and 20 years of age." Stephenson's account portrayed participants from ten to eighty years of age.

At least the *Watchman* was pretty much in line with its description of the group in the previous courthouse march as "virtually all" juveniles. Here's what Stephenson said when asked about this: "While it is true that the majority of those arrested with me were in their late teens and early twenties, what impressed me at the time was the large number of middle-aged and old folks, both male and female."

Beyond Stephenson's recollections and my earlier conclusion that the paper overstated the juvenile participation in the courthouse march, it seems that ninety percent—or about 270 out of 300—being sixteen to nineteen was a narrow window indeed. All things considered, it appears that this could possibly be another exaggeration.

The *Watchman* article poses that a dreaded factor had entered the picture for Greensboro. "National attention in the civil rights struggle continued to be focused on Greensboro at mid-week as city officials continued adamant in their refusal to permit the Negroes to stage a circuitous march through the town. . . ."

Demonstrators wanted to again march down Main Street and in front of the courthouse on their way to the burned church. Officials did not want a potential repeat of the previous courthouse scene so they took preemptive action by arresting and carting those demonstrators to Selma. Again, the *Greensboro Watchman* account was rather transparent.

The civil rights crowd, largely a bunch of noisy juveniles apparently more interested in silly antics than in anything else, gathered at the St. Matthew A.M.E. Church. . . . Mayor William C. Christian granted them a permit to march along North Street, to Tuscaloosa Street, and thence along this residential street four miles to the burned church. But they demanded the right to march through the business section of Greensboro, to the courthouse for a demonstration, thence up Centreville Street and over to Tuscaloosa Street before proceeding to the church. . . .

With the state troopers absent from the city, and only a handful of officers present, Mayor Christian refused this demand, and there the matter stood more than 48 hours later, at mid-day Wednesday. A road block was set up first at the intersection of Morse and Main streets, and then the next day moved northward about 75 yards on Morse street. . . .

A *New York Times* article about the tear gassing, "Tear Gas Halts 400 in Alabama March" reported that "Mayor W. C. Christian appealed tonight for help, and a force of state troopers was dispatched to Greensboro. . . ." Information gathered later indicated the numbers fluctuated from day to day, and the maximum was probably around 400. Arrival of the trooper force would seem to indicate that being undermanned could no longer hold up as a reason for disallowing the marchers' *demand*—a word with obvious emphasis in the *Watchman* report.

Consider that the road block was "moved northward about seventy-five yards on Morse street." The church is about two-thirds of the way down Morse Street, a very short town block even for Greensboro, with only a few homes facing the street; all were all occupied by black residents—if not demonstrators, probably supportive people. Moving the blockade northward from Main Street on this short block would have left 400 demonstrators very little room to maneuver outside the church building. Obviously, the authorities did not want them to set foot on Main Street toward the courthouse again. The *Watchman* portrayed an interesting scenario.

There demonstrators threatened to break over the barricade all Monday morning, and at 12:30 o'clock, the police turned tear gas on them. Several were immobilized from the gas, but most were back to the barricade within the hour. Shortly after 2 o'clock, a drenching rain fell. The Negroes, and some of the motley whites who have invaded this community, danced and sang in the rain, and some shed parts of their clothing. Late in the afternoon, both Monday and Tuesday, the demonstrators retired before dark, and appeared the next morning before 8 o'clock. The stalemate remained at this point early Wednesday afternoon. It was reported that NAACP lawyers were preparing to ask the federal courts for an injunction permitting the march. . . .

Of course, for "motley whites" like Stephenson to be portrayed as invaders is not surprising. Staying consistent in its reporting style that summer, the *Watchman* offered no elaboration on statements such as "threatened to break over the barrier." No other reason was directly given for the gassing, and—while heavy rain was reported—the *Watchman* could hardly be expected to editorially consider any potential connection to a holy event as did Stephenson.

Considering temperatures probably in the nineties at that time of year as well as cramped conditions, singing and dancing in the rain does not seem entirely unreasonable. Removing articles of clothing also isn't unreasonable considering the heat and tear gas, but the *Watchman* painted it all as akin to a drunken juvenile orgy. Maybe the account would seem more objective if it mentioned that gospel was the preferred form of singing—or even which parts of clothing were removed!

The *Times* gave a brief description of the gassing: "Canisters of tear gas flew through windows of the church and onto the parsonage next door. Most of the demonstrators drifted back to the church, but the gas was so thick in the church that they could not stay inside."

At any rate, authorities shipped the problem out of Greensboro, and where else would you move it but to Selma? The *Watchman* went on to address ongoing investigations into church burnings that led to those demonstrations, and its prejudicial approach is again transparent.

An investigation of the burning of the two Negro churches in Hale

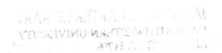

County continued this week, but apparently nothing developed. Some whites speculated that the churches, both of them small physically and low in membership, might easily have been sacrificed by civil righters so as to spur contributions from other parts of the country. There was also speculation as to why there was so little interest in the burning of a white church on the highway near Wedgworth. . . .

I have heard of a lot of fundraising approaches and have developed some myself, but burning churches is a new one to me. My follow-up research led me to believe that the burning of a white church was not just of little interest to national media but also to the *Watchman* since no further reports on it were published. Again, in the absence of facts about burned black churches, obviously overreaching white speculations are presented.

There were more attempts to march and more arrests that summer. The ones mentioned here provide a good idea of the way we Greensboro residents were spoon-fed information and a certain point of view about what happened. My youthful preconceptions about the civil rights movement and its participants in Greensboro were only strengthened by these filters.

Hamner Cobbs, the *Watchman* editor and feature writer, was a fiercely opinionated and widely respected professional whose influence extended far beyond my hometown. He was the great-grandson of the Reverend Nicholas Hamner Cobbs, appointed the first Episcopal Bishop of Alabama in 1844 at St. Paul's Episcopal Church in Greensboro. A slaveholder even as bishop, he nonetheless advocated good treatment of slaves as well as sharing the Christian message with them. He also vehemently opposed Alabama's secession from the union. Reportedly, he prayed that he would not live to see secession, and in one of the curious twists of the Civil War, the Alabama Convention's final vote approving secession was completed not long after Cobbs's death on the same day.

In 1943, Editor Cobbs revived the defunct Greensboro-based *Southern Watchman*, and edited it and the *Greensboro Watchman* simultaneously for a while. Under his leadership, the *Southern Watchman* took a strong stance in support of the Alabama Democratic Party. A March 10, 1943, *Tuscaloosa News* article entitled "The Southern Watchman Revived by Hamner Cobbs" reported that Cobbs specified the endorsement to include the party's white supremacist position.

In the white community of my day, Cobbs was known as an honest editor whose influence was used mostly for good. However, like me, he was part of a white-dominated culture where black people had long been considered inferior—a culture characterized by a powerful socialization process. Unlike me, Cobbs was central to one of the more important elements of that process—widespread public dissemination of information and opinion.

Socialization is the process by which people are absorbed into the behavior patterns and views of the culture surrounding them—as affected by family, peers, educational and religious organizations, media, etc. At its best, socialization contributes to a healthy community synergy for members to coexist together. At its worst, socialization fosters serious shared dysfunctions—usually assumed by members as normal. If a community member is rarely exposed to other points of view and/or is well conditioned to blindly defend the immediate culture's shared views, that person is unlikely to adopt new perspectives outside the insulated social structure—the bubble.

This does not negate the free will of people to determine their own actions and bear responsibility for outcomes, but people like Cobbs and me did live in a bubble of truly historic proportions. Dr. King and other leaders of the civil rights movement knew the tensile strength of our continually reinforced racial perspective. They knew how difficult it would be for us to change—that we were basically enslaved to those views.

The right to vote was subject to this intransigence. After the Civil Rights Act of 1957 made it clear that federal rather than state courts had jurisdiction over issues related to denial of voting rights, there was reason for an increased emphasis in the civil rights movement. This crystalized in 1961, and by 1962, a number of voter registration projects were underway in a number of states including Mississippi, Georgia, and Alabama. Sponsoring organizations included the NAACP, CORE, SCLC, and SNCC.

Despite all of the activities to register more black citizens, it was obvious that white leaders in many locations were still manipulating requirements in a way that maintained substantial restrictions on black citizens being able to vote. In 1964, a lot of resources were directed toward voter registration efforts in Mississippi. Related demonstrations and conflicts there were attracting media coverage. Violence toward activists was common. By 1965, the nation's attention was focused on Alabama—Birmingham, Montgomery, and Selma obviously central. However, marches also took place in smaller towns across the Black Belt area—including nearby Marion and Eutaw.

National attention and support was building for a broad stroke to be delivered. That happened when President Lyndon Baines Johnson signed the Voting Rights Act into law just some three weeks after I stood on that curb in Greensboro. It established that racial discrimination in voting and literacy requirements for voting were against the law in our nation. A number of reinforcing and monitoring provisions were also included that required periodic reauthorizations by Congress.

Unfortunately, five days after the Voting Rights Act was signed, the Watts riots broke out in Los Angeles. It was certainly contrary to the nonviolent principles of the civil rights movement as enunciated by its primary leaders. It definitely did not help me and like-minded white people I knew to witness fires and riots on television. Those scenes only reinforced our old stereotypes and fears of violent miles that would come if you gave *them* inches. Loaded with filters in regard to information processed in my mind, I was a product of my culture. In fact, my views and the powerful forces at work in me started long before I was born—in ways to be explored later. My conviction is that, as I stood on the curb that hot summer day, both the past and prospects for the future surrounded me.

4

MLK, KKK, and Mr. Smaw's Murder

One of the people drawing a lot of white barbershop fire in 1965 was the Reverend Martin Luther King. He had been in Greensboro early that summer, but I knew little about his brief visit—only hearing he wanted to stir up trouble. Later, I learned he was preparing people for voter registration efforts, including protests—the first occurring peacefully on July 6 when, according to a *New York Times* article the next day, about 450 black marchers first took the route from St. Matthew to the courthouse. They prayed and sang, but it all took place peacefully.

I don't know why I missed that first march. It may have taken place during one of my preparatory trips in advance of entering college that fall. I don't even recall hearing any talk about it. This may relate to the fact that it was peaceful, and white people thought it a passing nuisance. Also, maybe I hadn't gotten a haircut when the shop was abuzz with more than clippers. Prior to all the ensuing demonstrations, the word was that Dr. King probably made a hasty departure due to getting wind of a inhospitable reception planned for him by the Ku Klux Klan. I first heard this amidst big belly laughs at the barbershop. Later, I found something like that actually did happen to him in Greensboro, but in March 1968.

A 2002 *Tuscaloosa News* article reported on the incident.

> . . . the Reverend Martin Luther King Jr. made one of his common visits to this small Hale County city, but, on this evening, the Ku Klux Klan also paid a visit. As the men drove through town with their dome lights on and headlights off so the black populace could see their white robes and shotguns, Theresa Burroughs and her family hid King in their vacant home on Davis Street. There King slept overnight. He traveled to Selma the next day after the threat had passed. . . .

Only two weeks after this incident, Martin Luther King was killed in Memphis.

The house where Dr. King took refuge is now the Safe House Black History Museum. In recent times, Theresa Burroughs has been owner-manager of the Safe House, converting and managing it as a fascinating museum dedicated to preservation of the area's civil rights history. One of the marchers bearing down on me that summer day was Theresa Burroughs, although I didn't know her name at the time. She was quoted in the *News* article on her experiences in that and other demonstrations—quite direct and to the point of the matter, characteristic of her comments when I interviewed her for this book. "We were beaten, tear gassed, whipped, put in jail just because we pushed for the right to vote."

At a Los Angeles press conference on February 24, 1965, a reporter asked Dr. King a question about potential violence resulting from demonstrations and marches. His reply is quoted in the *Papers of Martin Luther King, Jr.* posted online by the Martin Luther King Research and Education Institute at Stanford University.

> When you get in a non-violent movement, the one thing that you commit yourself to is the fact that you are standing up for truth and justice and what is right, and you are willing to face death, if necessary. We teach this day in and day out that we must be willing to accept blows without retaliation—and we are constantly beaten in this movement—and we go to the point of saying that if physical death is the price that some must pay to free the white brothers and their children from a permanent psychological death and a permanent death of the spirit, then nothing can be more redemptive, so I would feel and certainly hope that if anything should happen to any of us in the non-violent movement, that Negroes would react to this as non-violently as they have to the mobs in Mississippi and Alabama.

Theresa Burroughs and others wanted the right to vote, but Dr. King seemed to say that it was also about freedom for that white guy on the curb, tire iron in hand. Today, I believe that and am thankful for it.

In Greensboro, for a few weeks following the July 1965 demonstrations, violence, church burnings, tear-gassing, and incarcerations, things were calm. Whites hoped for a return to normalcy and a retreat by outside media such as the *New York Times*. Alas, a few weeks after the Voting Rights bill became law on August 6, the *Times* found yet another reason for renewed focus when an elderly black man was found brutally beaten and left to die in his farm home just outside Greensboro. He was comatose for three days before dying on August 27, 1965.

Two characteristics of this crime magnified media attention. One was that the victim's tongue had been cut out. Also, according to law enforcement, there was an allegation (unsubstantiated) that operatives in the civil rights movement murdered the man for speaking out against their local activities. On the surface, it would seem likely the tongue cutting was indeed intended as a statement and/or silencer. Of course, another alternative could be to consider it the act of a mentally disturbed or extremely sadistic person or people.

Remarkably, the first time I knew of the murder was when I came across an Internet listing of what was labeled historical *lynchings* in the U.S. related to racism or bigotry. Published with no references, the list included a victim in Greensboro whose name was *Perry Small*. I was stunned to think someone could be lynched in my hometown of three thousand people without my awareness. I couldn't believe it was just another example of a blocked memory. I had to learn more. Following up with a website contact person, I was told that the source was *Racial and Religious Violence in America: A Chronology*, by Michael Newton and Judy Ann Newton.

The book is a fascinating and remarkably thorough historical compilation of religious and racial violence. Listed by year in the text, incidents are specified by type in the book's index. The Greensboro murder does not appear under *racial lynching*, but under *murder of blacks by whites*. The date is given as August 22, 1965, and the book states that "Perry Small, an elderly black man, is found beaten to death in his home with his tongue cut out."

Michael Newton also wrote a highly acclaimed book on the Ku Klux Klan, *The Invisible Empire*. I contacted Newton, who was very helpful. He told me that his "Perry Small" source was a 1965 article in the *New York Times*.

I had trouble locating the *Times* article. On microfilm, there were three different *Greensboro Watchman* articles covering the event, investigation, and trial that followed. The first appeared Thursday, August 26, after discovery of the critically injured man the previous Sunday, a day after the attack reportedly occurred on Saturday, August 21. The front-page headline was, "Negro, 89, victim of brutal attack." His name was given as Perry *Smaw*, not Small.

The *Watchman* reported that Smaw was found in his bedclothes in a pool of blood by out-of-town relatives who came to visit him that Sunday morning. The article further stated that two black suspects had been arrested (one of the suspects apparently was later released and never charged). According to a deputy sheriff, Smaw was beaten into unconsciousness with an iron skillet. The tongue-cutting was reported in brief but gruesome detail. "Apparently, the assailants pulled his tongue as far from the mouth as they could and cut it off with a knife or other sharp instrument. . . ."

The article went on to reflect on the investigation, assuming a connection between the assault and the civil rights activities in Hale County, "especially in view of the brutal manner in which his tongue was cut from his mouth. It is understood that Smaw had been outspoken in opposition to some of the methods employed by the younger Negroes in the movement, and that they were using this method in silencing him."

In a later edition, the *Watchman* reported that a black man by the name of Long had confessed. The same report said that Smaw died without being able to identify his assailant, and added the following observation:

> The Smaw case, because of the aged man's outspoken criticism of the Civil Rights Movement, attracted nation-wide attention. Local authorities did not put their finger directly on the civil rights affair as a motive, but Long is alleged to have been under pressure to join the movement, and there were indications that he had been threatened by that group.

After considering the context here and in other articles, I concluded there was an editorial mistake that Smaw, not Long, was the one alleged to have been pressured to join the movement, which at least would have been consistent with "indications" that Smaw had been threatened. As with previous articles, the newspaper listed no source for these allegations and indications. Given the entire scenario and my awareness of the reporting trends, I think it likely that the efforts to connect Smaw's murder and the civil rights movement were unfounded and prejudicial.

According to reports, there was a confession from Long within a week. Some money was missing from Smaw's house, and Long led authorities to items he took from there: a rifle, a silver dollar, and a butcher knife—the latter allegedly used to cut out Smaw's tongue. Needless to say, with a confession and weapon, conviction was assured. The final *Watchman* article on the subject revealed that Long received a life sentence. Case closed—yet the circumstances and allegations surrounding all this were so odd they provoked my continued concern. I wanted to find other news articles that clarified what turned out to be unfounded allegations. I also wanted to know what Smaw's family thought about the court's finding as to guilt and motive.

I eventually found three *New York Times* articles on Smaw's death. The articles maintained the victim's name as "Perry Small." The first, dated August 26, was titled "Negro In Alabama Found Mutilated," and had a revealing subtitle, "Lost Tongue for Opposing Rights Drive, Officer Says."

It cited statements of Chief Deputy Sheriff David Holloway to the effect that two suspects were arrested and that the victim had been heard "making strong statements against civil rights demonstrations on August 14th on a Greensboro street. He said he believed that Small was mutilated and beaten to discourage other Negroes from opposing the civil rights movement."

Obviously, the *Times* reported a more direct assertion by the deputy than had the *Watchman*. Gilbert Slay, vice president of the Hale County Improvement Association, was quoted as stating the two arrested had nothing to do with the movement though they might have been sympathetic, also saying that "Holloway is trying to blame everything on the movement. . . ." The article later said Holloway discounted "robbery as a motive," even though a rifle and money were missing.

I could find no additional information on allegations tying the crime to the civil rights movement in any future *Watchman* or *Times* murder or trial coverage. Regarding the family's opinions on Smaw's murder and the motive, I found a relevant article in the September 16, 1965, edition of

Jet, "Alabama Victim's Kin Sees Robbery, Not Rights As Motive". Smaw's grandson, the Reverend Edward Small, was quoted saying that he felt robbery was the motive, and that it had nothing to do with "any alleged outspoken opposition to civil rights demonstrations." As for the Smaw-Small name variation, I located a member of Smaw's family who now has the name Small. However, he could not provide any information on what appeared to be a name change. While I do not know for sure, it could have been a choice based on Smaw having been a slave-holding plantation family name that was applied to ancestors in slavery. Such a choice faced more black families than I want to consider—one of the tragic outcomes of slavery I came across when undertaking the daunting task of finding the roots of my family's relationships with black people. Suffice to say for now that the anonymity with which I regarded black people (by not caring to know them by name) is overshadowed by the way many blacks were denied their own names in slavery and on official records.

In the final analysis, everything indicated that blame for Smaw's murder rightly belonged to a thief and that neither the civil rights movement nor my hometown was to blame. While some may think that exposing false allegations and the mistakes that followed is enough to conclude the matter, I disagree. My hometown—regardless of its history of racism—does not deserve to be associated with a racial lynching if it did not happen, and I communicated that with Newton about his book citing the murder as a racially motivated white-on-black crime. He graciously acknowledged the mistake, and said he would be glad to act as a reference for any inquiry about it. I also attempted to convey this mistake to the website that posted the murder as a racial lynching but found it to be published by an anonymous entity, and I could not locate the contact person with whom I had previously spoken. Surely, this meant the end of my pursuit of the matter, but no—it was the case that would not go away.

I inadvertently came across something published online many years after the murder. It attempted to resurrect the discounted speculation that Smaw's alleged criticism of the civil rights movement resulted in his death. The source was obviously radical and unreliable. I dismissed it and chose not to dignify it by giving its name. However, all of this does illustrate that speculations—whether in a small-town newspaper, on the web, or in this and other books—can easily be promoted or manipulated for any number of purposes. Sources do need to be confirmed and speculative statements should be identified as such.

Verifying information was not so easy in my hometown where, in this case, the media and at least one law enforcement official were either slanting or speculating. This treatment (strengthened by such things as distorted barbershop buzz) meant even the more objective white residents in Greensboro had little chance of attributing nobility or justice to the civil rights movement, its objectives, and activities.

5

Jail Blues, Boy on Horseback, Leopard's Spots

L ike most children, I was somewhat isolated from the trauma that followed in my family and in our little community as I was growing up. My life was full of mystery and energy with much laughter and tears—really a fairly healthy mix. As the sun sank behind the county jail across the street on hot summer evenings, I enjoyed lying on my back in front-yard clover—occasionally listening to prisoners make music. When one particularly talented but obviously troubled prisoner was in residence (frequently due to excessive drinking and related behaviors), I enjoyed the tones of a blues harmonica, both haunting and soothing under the night stars.

Prisoners were predominantly black. In my pre-adolescence, I liked to meander over to the jail for various reasons, including partaking of the best scuppernongs that ever curled through a tall barbed wire-topped fence. I ate them right off the vine. My friends and I also had great fun throwing things into a burning garbage pile just outside the fence. When a light bulb exploded in the fire, leaving me with a lifelong scar—I avoided disaster by the literal blink of an eye—I gave up this activity, probably at my mother's insistence. Boys were boys, and we did things like that in those days. I shudder to think about my grandchildren doing such things today!

Black prisoners often watched my foolishness from the barred windows in the jail, but they never spoke to me much; they were black and I was a white boy, a difference that mattered, in jail or not. Another reason for their silence is that when he was a deputy sheriff, my father gained a reputation for administering consequences to black men who did not "stay in their places." He also controlled payroll for a lot of black workers under his plant management, so these men had reason to be respectful to the boss's young son (whether the son deserved it or not). On a few occasions an inmate broke the silence by asking me to please ask "Mr. John" to get him out of there. I always passed it on, and it always fell on deaf ears, to my knowledge.

I have always been intrigued by a photograph of my dad at age six or seven—a profile of him sitting astride a beautiful black stallion. He is wearing a white outfit, from lace collar to shoes—including white riding pants. He's holding the reins, but someone else dutifully holds the bit in the horse's mouth. Facing the camera at relaxed attention, the attendant is a black man appearing to be in his fifties, with white shirt and suspenders, looking very much the part of a gentleman's servant.

My father lived his youthful years in relative luxury. However, the little boy pictured atop the magnificent horse does not look happy. I know that people did not smile as much for photographers back then, but to me this particular picture symbolizes the sometimes unkind lot of prosperity—with him as its victim. My father was a smart man and a math whiz, but he had only a ninth-grade education. He did not finish high school because he was considered incorrigible—even after being sent to the prestigiously strict Barton Academy in Mobile upon getting the boot from prestigiously strict Southern Academy in Greensboro. My father was a rouser raised with the thought that he was better than others. Failure is commonplace and often a prerequisite to success, but when expectation exceeds affirmation in a child's formative years, a lifetime of struggle can be the outcome. Real happiness and contentment eluded my father for much of his life.

Our family church was not going to help my father along the lines of humility, certainly not pertaining to black people, as illustrated by a sermon at the Greensboro Presbyterian Church when I was about ten. It pertained to a Bible reference in the Old Testament, Jeremiah 3:13: "Can the Ethiopian change his skin, or the leopard his spots? [then] may ye also do good, that are accustomed to do evil."

While not entirely direct, the sermon left no room for doubt, even in my young mind, about the minister's intent for our hearts. It was a metaphorical application to a black person's skin and nature. He was saying the black person could never change his skin color or become equal to a white person.

I do not recall any other sermon at the church, but this one had some memorable markers. It was unusually dynamic and produced an uncommonly enthusiastic response. Most sermons were sleep-inducing for me. This one was punctuated with exclamation points! There were even a few audible (and traditionally rare) "Amens!" from the audience, and there were high praises and vigorous handshakes for the minister afterwards.

Cultures are largely self-protective. When cultural values are under attack, beliefs will be reinforced: And our cultural belief was that black people did not fit in with white people. To a white boy growing up in Greensboro, the minister's message made perfect sense. Today, when I read that passage, I see it as pure irony, especially when I consider its broader context about having misplaced trust in lies to a point of no return.

> Can the Ethiopian change his skin, or the leopard his spots? [then] may ye also do good, that are accustomed to do evil. Therefore will I scatter them as the stubble that passeth away by the wind of the wilderness. This [is] thy lot, the portion of thy measures from me, saith the LORD; because thou hast forgotten me, and trusted in falsehood.

Wayne Flynt, in his book Alabama Baptists: Southern Baptists in the Heart of Dixie (University of Alabama Press, 1998), explained that such manipulations of scripture were common. "Although much can be made of the way in which southern culture ensnared white Baptists, the truth is that its tentacles were strong enough to ensnare Methodists, Presbyterians, Episcopalians, and Catholics as well."

My father was not at church for the leopard's-spots sermon that he would have thoroughly appreciated. My mother consistently attended, but I recall only a few times when he did. He allowed his money to be contributed to the church formerly pastored by his grandfather, but he spoke of the hypocrisy of some members as if it justified his absence.

He may have been right sometimes about individuals, but judging others could well have contributed to his near lifelong lack of humility. For too much of his life, my father felt he was a failure; that he couldn't measure up or be "better than them" in the broader application of my grandmother's whisper. Accepting an alternative was hard for him, even when severe crises came upon the family. He turned to alcohol as an old friend rather than to family, friends, church, or God. Trusting in lies as the scripture indicated, his spots were difficult to change, especially as to racial views. Years later, he did develop a broader view of others (not uncommon as a person ages). I'm not sure if he changed his views on race, but sometimes generations simply must pass.

6

FIRESTORMS, PRANKS, WALLACE, FEARS, AND DOGS DEGRADED

Highly significant events in the civil rights movement followed Rosa Parks's refusal to give up a bus seat to a white man in Montgomery late in 1955 and Martin Luther King Jr.'s associated emergence as a national leader. One such event was the 1957 desegregation of Central High School in Little Rock, Arkansas. Governor Faubus ordered the National Guard to stop black students from entering the high school. A court injunction cleared the way, but when a thousand white residents turned out to force removal of the students, President Eisenhower ordered in a division of the Army and federalized the National Guard. A media firestorm followed.

Less than a year later, on one of our rushed family vacations, we stayed a few days in Little Rock just because my father considered the school to be a sort of shrine to brave people defending segregation. At age twelve, I stood with him in front of Central High, thinking there was something sacred about that place. Not only was it the biggest high school I had ever seen, but it stood as another stone symbol of pride in a way of life under attack. At that point, I did not think that Greensboro High would ever be integrated. Integration was still just something that happened elsewhere—not in my town or my state.

Back in Alabama, in 1963, Reverends King, Shuttlesworth, and Abernathy fanned the flames in Birmingham with a march that resulted in newspaper and television images seen around the world and imprinted in the minds of Americans—Bull Connor, snarling police dogs, and terrorized children. That was followed by the historic march on Washington where King's "I Have a Dream" speech was broadcast across the country. Like so many others in Greensboro, I was sneering at it all but still carrying the indelible image of those menacing Birmingham dogs.

By 1965, everything turned toward the Voting Rights Act, including demonstrations like those in Greensboro that challenged voter eligibility laws and registration barriers. But it had little effect on me.

During those years, white rural Alabama youth were insulated, and we acted as teenagers did: we enjoyed the usual small-town drag racing on a straight country stretch, and some of us went from our *dry* county to an adjacent *wet* county to get beer. We would often find some older man to go with us or pay an adult hanging around outside to go in the club or store and get what we wanted.

Despite a lot of drinking in my family background, I was an occasional light drinker. Truth be known, even when a little intoxicated and generating occasionally loud bravado, my friends and I were relatively harmless. Like a lot of teenage boys, I was emboldened when with a group of my peers. We craved excitement, and sometimes, probably in an attempt to relieve our small-town boredom, one of us would get a really harebrained idea. Everyone then reacted like piranhas to fresh meat. Mostly, it was harmless stuff of the basically stupid variety, but occasionally, we would cross the line.

Once, someone had the brilliant idea that we should find some really dynamic and different way to utilize cases of empty Coke bottles. We foraged around town for them late one Saturday night, not knowing the target, only that we would use the bottles as grenades in some way. Sometimes, we would hang out of moving cars and blast road signs, but this time, we were incited to do something bigger.

There were five or six of us, and somebody said we should chunk our missiles over a cliff and down upon the unsuspecting enemy sleeping in their camp below—namely, black families in their tin-roofed houses. As we drove to the roadside above those homes, our enthusiasm rose. We all stepped outside the car armed with bottles, and unleashed our attack on the count of three. We threw bottle after bottle until there were none left. They exploded and ricocheted off the tin roofs, rudely interrupting the still of that night. We could hear startled shouts and screams from below, and we yelped and yowled in return, delirious with joy, before we jumped back in the car and burned rubber down that two-lane paved road.

No matter how much we craved excitement, we would never have done that if white people had lived in those houses. Something within me took morbid pleasure in the fact that they were *niggers*. Yes, we were typical teenagers taking a cheap shot to get a thrill in a small town, but there was more to it. We saw the black families living their lives peacefully at the bottom of that roadside cliff as objects and nothing more. They didn't deserve our respect. The barrage of bottles surely struck fear into the hearts of the shocked adults in the houses and interrupted the sweet dreams of their children. It's an experience from my youth that is difficult for me to recall—or write about.

More than the usual prank, the assault seemed to feed a hungering anger in our bellies. It was how we were socialized, and I and some—if not all—of my friends enjoyed the position symbolized by being atop that cliff with *them* down below. We never heard that anyone reported our bottle-throwing incident to the police. We didn't want to get caught, of course, but we had good reason to believe that even if the crime had been reported, the worst response would have been a verbal rebuke. A similar assault on the homes of white families would have had dire consequences—and we were smart enough to know that.

A year or so before the bottle-throwing incident, I was riding in an older friend's truck late one night after we had had a few beers. Like in most small towns across America, teenagers in Greensboro enjoyed cruising the town. That particular night, we spotted a black man—probably in his fifties—walking just off the side of the road. He had a noticeable limp. My friend pulled over behind him, and turned his headlights on high beam. The gentleman turned around and squinted into the lights, straining to make out the truck and its occupants. My friend said, "Watch this." He grabbed his rifle from the rack behind him and got out of the car. I hurriedly said, "Wait a minute! Wait a minute!" Throwing bottles at houses was one thing. Aiming a gun at a man was altogether different, and even then and as a teenage socialized racist I knew that.

He pointed his rifle at the man, stepped into the headlight beam, and shouted, "I'm gonna shoot you, nigger!"

I felt—I hoped—he was kidding, but I was still shocked. The black man shouted back, "Don't shoot me! My leg hurts!"

In response, my friend started laughing uncontrollably. He bent over holding his stomach, and dropped the rifle barrel toward the ground. I grabbed his arm and told him we needed to get out of there. By the time we got back in the truck, the black man had run into the trees beside the road.

As he drove me home, my friend said it was just a joke, but I was unnerved by the whole incident, and I distanced myself from him after that night. In one way, his treatment of the man was no different from how any of us treated black folks: as if they had no worth whatsoever. I held a similar view at the time, but at least my conscience was somewhat functional. However, I don't think there was anything highly noble or meritorious about my protesting; I would probably have done the same had my friend threatened to shoot a dog on the side of the road. The idea of playing a joke by threatening the life of a man you did not even know just because he was black is horrendous. Even though I grew to recognize my own socialization as a racist, I still feel shame at my role in activities that amounted to sheer persecution. The lyrics of the marchers' song spoke about many of us then, regardless of age or cause: We were blind, and we needed to see.

It was only two years before the march of 1965 that Governor George Wallace gained national notoriety by blocking a doorway to ceremonially protest the registration of the University of Alabama's first black students, Vivian Malone and James Hood. I shook hands with George Wallace once—he had a powerful and memorable grip. A former Golden Gloves champion boxer, he was truly a tough person.

He was also a skilled politician whose primary objective was probably pure politics, not, as is usually assumed, to stand in that schoolhouse door for a principle—whether segregation or states' rights. In his book, *Cradle of Freedom*, Frye Gaillard portrayed the heroism of low-profile people who promoted the civil rights movement in Alabama. He also portrayed subtleties involved in the thinking and motivations of some of the more infamous personalities such as Wallace. As a young circuit judge, Wallace was not known for the segregationist positions he later took as governor. In fact, Gaillard points out that black civil rights attorney J. L. Chestnut called

Circuit Judge Wallace "the most liberal judge I had ever practiced in front of. He was the first judge in Alabama to call me 'Mister' in his courtroom."

I remember thinking as a youth that Wallace was a real fighter for Alabama, a bulldog battling the unrighteous foes of states' rights and segregation. That view was shared by many white people in Alabama and other places as well. Wallace himself cultivated the image of a segregationist as he saw historic events unfolding that provided him with the opportunity to gain a distinctive spotlight. He then capitalized on fear and rode the image all the way to national prominence and the presidential primaries in 1968 and 1972.

Though some may have had principled positions on states' rights, the resistance of most whites to blacks exercising their rights was more a matter of racism and fear than it was of high principle. Fear is not so hard to understand in the context of history, including the horror of slavery and the existence of groups like the KKK. What if blacks had equal access and rights, including the all-important right to vote? Wouldn't they turn the tables?

While not every black person experienced every oppressive treatment in the South in the twentieth century, many black people were hounded by white mobs, the KKK, and unfair law enforcement officers and judges. In general, they were denied rights—some were bombed, burned, and shot to death. Shadows of slave rebellion and Nat Turner rose up, and—consciously or subconsciously—we whites allowed our ancient fears and new ones to be reinforced by those in power, leaders either seeking their own selfish ends or enslaved by fear themselves. Poverty and crime exacerbated fear, and the ancient force was nurtured in the bubble right up to the day I stood on the street curb with tire iron raised—prideful and fearful.

During Wallace's initial 1958 campaign for governor, as Gaillard put it, he "stared at the camera during one of his ads, his dark eyes softer than they would seem later on, and he declared with an evident sense of conviction: "I want to tell the good people of this state . . . if I didn't have what it took to treat a man fair regardless of the color of his skin, then I don't have what it takes to be the governor of your great state."

Whatever Wallace's personal convictions at any time in his life, he was definitely a politician who danced to the tunes that elected him. He went from Golden Gloves champion to circuit judge to governor to candidate for president—then to a wheelchair when he was shot campaigning. During the years of his disability, he indicated considerable awareness of his wrongs, and renounced anything he did that was harmful to black people. What I know about Wallace makes me think he sincerely regretted his racism. He was just another man who had been blind and then could see. I like to think part of his regret involved a past lust for power. His attitude of repentance could be appropriate for a number of politicians.

Those snarling German shepherd police dogs biting at protestors in Birmingham were not the only dogs affected by racism. Rin was our family dog from the beginning of my conscious memories. He lived to be fourteen or fifteen years old, and I was one grieving ninth-grader when we found his body under the house, beneath my bedroom where he always slept. My father named him after Rin Tin Tin, a German shepherd television star. Rin Tin Tin was a law enforcement dog whose only canine TV competitor was the more theatrical and gentle farm dog, Lassie, a collie. Our Rin was a collie, but I think my father wanted him to be more like an aggressive police dog than a gentle farm dog—thus, the name.

The original Rin Tin Tin was a real-life hero with military service in wartime, and his legacy extended through his descendants. Believe it or not, my father once told me that our Rin was descended from Rin Tin Tin. He later said it was a joke, but I think he relished the idea, similar to his assertion that our family was descended from Queen Elizabeth I. He also once told a friend, unbeknownst to me until later, that I was studying medicine in college, which was not even close to my chosen field. You might say he was inclined to contorting facts with fantasy, especially when it came to status-related matters. It was mostly harmless, and perhaps his being "better than them" required it.

Rin was gentle, loyal, protective to a flaw—but my beloved dog also engaged in racist practices. My father sent him to a guard dog training camp in Georgia, and as a result, he did not take kindly to strangers coming into our yard. If we knew an unfamiliar adult was coming, we chained our protective dog to a wire clothesline attached to two trees beside the house so he could run back and forth but not attack. When the visitor arrived, Rin would bark viciously and run up and down the length of the clothesline, jumping and twirling around as some dogs do. But when the visitor was black, Rin's behavior kicked into a frenzy. I once saw him bite a chunk out of an unannounced black visitor's pants. I knew that any unknown black person risked serious injury by appearing unannounced in our yard. Despite his loud barking, Rin normally stayed at a distance when the stranger was a white person.

I remember taking pride in Rin's discriminating ferocity, and my father said it was due to an ingrained sense the dog had about black people—of course, a noble trait. Later, I considered that either Rin's formal training was oriented that way, or he picked it up through the dispositions of my father and me, maybe both. For all I know, given my father's law enforcement career, Rin was trained at the same place as the Birmingham dogs.

Either way, it is a shame to think that noble and loyal animals would be trained or conditioned to absorb discrimination on the basis of skin color. I think perhaps Rin was not unlike many of us conditioned into racism—except that we humans are blessed with the capacity to reason and change. Whites who thought Rin's behavior toward blacks was inherent and/or noble were dead wrong. He and the dogs of Birmingham were naturally inclined toward nobility, and they deserved better than to serve humanity's ancient fears.

7

JFK, Offer to Kill, Key
and King at the Barbershop

W hite people in Greensboro were not cruel or inhuman by nature. However, a few years before the march, I and a lot of Greensboro High School students could have been considered inhuman (as well as typically immature) due to what happened on November 22, 1963. That day, I was just another bored sixteen-year-old sitting in the first class after lunch. Class members were finally settling down after a few latecomers ambled in. Generally I enjoyed classes, but my mind often drifted to football or girls. The beginning of a blissful daydream had just begun when it was interrupted by a message on the intercom. It was the unmistakable, militaristic voice of our principal—even more solemn than usual—calling all students and staff to an assembly.

At the assembly, Principal Jim Key (always Coach to us) announced that President Kennedy had been killed. Not a small number of kids broke into spontaneous applause and shouts of glee. Some of it could have been premeditated because I later found that many had already heard the rumor. I don't remember applauding, but honestly I cannot recall what I thought or did at the time. Most of the culprits were boys, and it would not have been out of character then for me to have joined in. Key, whose disciplinary coaching style carried over into his new job, soundly rebuked us as only he could. He said, whether we agreed with him or not, John Kennedy was our president. Being joyful was reason for pure shame. He then led us in prayer for the president's family and for our nation.

President Kennedy was shot at 12:30 p.m., Central Standard Time, and pronounced dead at 1 p.m. I didn't feel bad about our president being assassinated. He was one of those bad-mouthed by just about everyone I knew, ranking just above Martin Luther King and maybe Fidel Castro in our Hall of Shame as one of the worst threats to common decency and the fabric of our nation. We knew that fabric was based south of the Mason-Dixon line. It was a sacred line that had been violated one hundred years earlier by bluecoats—folks like Lincoln, Grant, and Sherman. Our view was that they led a movement to desecrate a way of life, our way of life, and destroy the pride of good people. It was not just that we lost a war, but that we were made to suffer insults for so many years afterwards. In our minds, Kennedy was just another leader continuing the persecution and desecration.

Of course, verbal or nonverbal, my response to Kennedy's death, and the response of most around me, was totally inappropriate and shameful. Richard Stephenson, the white man who had taken part in one of the Greensboro demonstrations, as I noted earlier, told me about the response of those around him. "Most people up north were devastated by the assassination, and were appalled by the images on television and in the newspapers of some people cheering his death. Kennedy represented hope to lots of people, and, as much as he was a consummate politician, folks were somehow inspired by the image of sophistication and intellectual depth that he (and his entourage) projected. . . ."

Stephenson admitted that he's now doubtful about some aspects of Kennedy's legacy, but for many whites I knew in Greensboro at the time, there was no doubt. We found nothing redeeming about President Kennedy, even in memoriam. I am glad our principal was an honorable man of faith who gave his due respect by rebuking us and publicly praying for the Kennedy family and for our nation. And even though I didn't see it then, I now understand that Coach Key diminished my armor of socialized racism with his actions that day. As will become apparent, the same man subsequently challenged white mainstream Greensboro through his direct role in dealing with integration.

My father was not a politician, and he had no room for negotiation on race relations. His reputation with a blackjack and brass knuckles was well-established, and it would not be an overstatement to say he was feared by just about everyone who might cross him, especially black men. Not that I had any evidence for it, but I always thought he might have beaten someone to death.

Once, when I was a boy, a black man drove his car from a side street out in front of our car, forcing my father to slam on the brakes. No one was hurt and the cars weren't damaged, but the black man knew what he'd done, and he took off. With me in the car and my father spouting a steady stream of cuss words, we chased that car for miles out into the country. Finally, the offender's car careened off the side of a dirt road into a ditch, and he scrambled out to run. My father leapt out and did a full sprint trying to catch the guy. I knew my father carried brass knuckles, and I saw him reaching for them before disappearing into the wooded area where the man fled.

I was frozen to the passenger seat. When my father came back, he was huffing and puffing and only said that the guy got away. He turned the car around, and we headed back to town in silence. He was brooding. Later that night, I overheard him telling my mother that he and the sheriff rode back to the spot where the man had left the car. He said the car and the man were nowhere in sight. He did not seem worried one bit, and nothing more was ever said about the incident. I had no doubt that, if my father had caught him, that man would have suffered a beating and could have been killed. If the man had been white, I don't think any of that would have happened.

My father had a black man working for him to do all types of odd jobs requiring sheer brawn. This right-hand man was over six feet tall, very strong, and not much of a talker. He walked with a slight limp from an unidentified malady. He also had an unswerving devotion to my father whom he called Mr. John, as did all the other black people in town.

As a young boy, I occasionally walked down Main Street with my father. Once, this right-hand man walked with us—or I should say behind—probably to carry something. We passed a black teenager, probably seventeen or eighteen, who did not move readily aside from my father's path, not giving the customary right of way, and brushed against him just slightly. My father looked back at him disdainfully. The right-hand man stepped up and spoke to my father in hushed tones as if not wanting me to hear, but I heard.

He said, "Mr. John, you want me to kill him?"

My father replied with a wave of his hand, "nah," and that was that. Serious or not, in that moment, a few words expressed the sense of dominance that was continually fed to me in one way or another.

An October 13, 2002, *Tuscaloosa News* article, "Politics of Color," by Thomas Spencer, reflected on the election of Artur Davis, a black man, to Congress. A big part of Davis's platform pertained to economic development in the Black Belt that included nine counties in his district, Hale County being one. The unusual thing about the Davis platform was not that he espoused developing the area economically. It was that he emphasized the message of working together to reach goals important to both blacks and whites in the depressed region. This was a stark contrast to his incumbent opponent's campaign that had focused primarily on garnering the majority black vote.

Davis, who graduated magna cum laude from Harvard University and cum laude from Harvard Law School, won the election with a combination of black and white votes. At the time, Barack Obama's name barely registered on voters' radar so the fact that he was a classmate of Davis was not a factor.

Later, when Davis made a run to become the Democratic candidate for governor, he was defeated when he dared to take some stands contrary to traditional black Democratic leadership in Alabama. At any rate, Artur Davis's election to Congress was certainly unprecedented, and, in his article, Spencer proposed that a major change may have taken place. Perhaps it denoted a shift, a new political reality. He said some believe that, "Politics in the Black Belt doesn't have to be a power struggle between the races." This proposition ran against the grain of many years of racial polarization in Black Belt politics.

A quote in the article really took my mind back to that walk down Main Street with my father and his so-called right-hand man. Perry County Commissioner Albert Turner Jr. said whites in his area "don't want progress. They don't believe that black people have sense enough to run government. . . . In their world, they wish it was back in the 1940s or 1950s when, if a white man was walking down the street, you had to get off the sidewalk. They don't believe we can walk together."

Talk about a flashback! I remembered the question, "Do you want me to kill him, Mr. John?," and immediately sat down to write a note to Congressman Davis. Without any details, I simply wished him the very best of success in bringing people together for the common good. Maybe the county commissioner in Perry County did not accurately reflect what was going on in the minds of white people there, or maybe Hale County or Greensboro was different. I did not know.

I hope leaders, black and white, with the same vision as Davis will be successful in bringing people together. On reading that *Tuscaloosa News* article, I hoped little white boys in Greensboro were able to see black and white citizens walking together on the sidewalk—talking about their families, about community concerns, and about building the community up together—rather than being preoccupied with such nonsensical things as their relative places on the sidewalk.

The long-term football coach at Greensboro High was Jim Key, the same man who later rebuked us as our principal when JFK was killed. His reputation as a winner and a tough-but-fair character builder was well-established by the time he left to assume a college coaching job. Also a Baptist deacon, he was considered a community leader. After Key left, we had two head coaches in less than a year. The first had a drinking problem that showed. He got the quick kick out of town. The second coach was a nice guy and disciplinarian in the Key mold, but he was gone almost as quickly as the other guy—of his own volition, but I don't know why.

Given the roller-coaster ride with coaches, everyone was down. Then, all of a sudden, Jim Key returned like a knight in shining armor. I think he did not particularly like college coaching. There may have been other reasons, but it did not matter. Everyone on the team and in town was just plain tickled pink about it. The barbershop glowed! Unfortunately, as a sophomore, I broke my arm in a scrimmage game. With healing complicated by unruly diabetes, I became discouraged and did not play the game I loved any more in high school. Still, Coach Jim Key instilled much-needed focus and discipline in me—as he did for many others during his career. Discipline for something you love is a great thing, and so is standing up for what you believe, as Jim Key showed us through President Kennedy's death.

The summer after my freshman year at the University of Alabama was my last full summer in Greensboro. Our senior class had been the last segregated one, and by that summer of 1966, integration had run a full school year at my Alma Mater. One day, I went to the barbershop for a haircut. The buzz among men there was all about someone who had apparently gone off the deep end. The crowd might as well have been in chorus together as they repeatedly said such things as, "He just went crazy! Has he completely lost his mind?" Turns out they were extremely disappointed in this man. I was shocked to learn the object of their dismay was Jim Key. I did not know what he had done, but those men were downright angry in a perplexed way. In contrast to its previous jubilant glow over Key returning to Greensboro as coach, the barbershop crowd was now red hot with scorn and bewilderment over his actions and words as the school's principal in support of integration.

In view of how Key had handled our response to Kennedy's death, I was not as shocked as the barbershop crew. However, considering my still-racist view, it was strange that I did not feel angry. Yet it took years before I realized the nature of this confused, even conflicted, reaction by those men. Key's barbershop assailants were unlikely to have ever confronted him personally, and they knew him too well to portray him as a plotting villain—so he had to be crazy! After the barbershop incident, I could not consign Key to some vague notion of insanity or to evil motives. Maybe he was sincerely wrong. In time, I came to believe that Coach Key just dared to do what was right, from his resounding rebuke of our class to his cooperation with integration. I don't know if he ever regained the respect of the white community overall, but surely many others came to view him as I did over time. He made a difference for me, not only in terms of focus and discipline, but also in standing up for what is right—and facing the stark truth about myself and my view of others.

The barbershop was the same place where I had, the previous summer and before the march, seen a remarkable black and white photograph. It appeared to be a copied newspaper clipping, with a caption beneath reading "Consorting with Known Communists." The setting was a classroom. A small group of assembled men were being lectured. The lecturer was easily recognized as Cuban dictator Fidel Castro.

A man brought the picture in, pointed and said, "Do you see who that is, right there in the front row?"

"*King,*" people kept repeating with scowls and expletives as it moved through all hands. When it came to me, I could see that it was indeed Reverend Martin Luther King, or so it seemed. He wore a tie-less white shirt and was attentively leaning forward in his chair. Talk about a barber-shop buzzing! The cacophony of voices and sheer vitriol of the crowd was unparalleled from my experience in this place. The primary figure in the struggle for civil rights in the 1960s was undoubtedly Dr. Martin Luther King. He said and did important things, bringing attention to the need for definitive action on civil rights injustices. However, I still occasionally hear people demeaning him based on questions about his character or associating him directly with violent episodes during the sixties or with entitlement principles or patronizing of black people.

A lot of negative speculations were generated about King by his detrac-tors. A *Final Report Concerning Dr. Martin Luther King, Jr.* was done by the Congressional Select Committee to Study Governmental Operations. It was dated April 23, 1976, and this appeared in the report:

> On July 12, 1963, Governor Ross E. Barnett of Mississippi testified before the Senate Commerce Committee that civil rights legislation was "a part of the world Communist conspiracy to divide and conquer our country from within." Barnett displayed a photograph entitled "Martin Luther King at Communist Training School" taken by an informant for the Georgia Commission of Education, which showed Dr. King at a 1957 Labor Day Weekend seminar at the Highlander Folk School in Monteagle, Tennessee with three individuals whom he alleged were com-munists. When Senator Mike Monroney challenged the accuracy of this characterization, Barnett stated that he had not checked the allegations with the FBI and suggested that the Commerce Committee do so. The FBI subsequently concluded that the charges were false.

Long after King's death, I heard people associate him and the civil rights movement with Communism. Investigations over the course of history since, by public and private entities, have shown no substantial connection—though the report cited here and others verified attempts by Communists to infiltrate. While Dr. King may have had some personal shortcomings, he was the chosen vessel of the civil rights movement, and his heroic image was earned the hard way. The barbershop piranha-like photo response demonstrated that King's chances to be judged objectively by whites in Greensboro were nil. However, in a funny way, my experience over the barbershop photograph set the stage for me to begin to associate him with Coach Jim Key as my thinking matured.

While it may be in the nature of some human beings to have needs met by considering themselves better than other human beings in extreme ways, that is not the only cause for racism in its different forms. The unique form of racism on display at the courthouse and the barbershop certainly did not start in the mid-twentieth century. It did not begin there in my family, either. Mine goes back to a long line of ancestral pride and the unique nature of antebellum times in the Black Belt, a history rooted in cotton. Understanding my related family history provides insights, not only into my racist disposition, but also that of an entire culture.

8

THE TREASURE

A familiar guardian overlooked the gathering of demonstrators that summer day when I stood holding the tire iron. The stone Confederate foot soldier stood erect: cap perfectly straight on his head, rifle butt resting between his feet at the base, hands grasping the barrel, staring dead ahead. I spent many days as a child playing around that memorial statue. For me, demonstrators had no place beneath the oak trees in the courthouse yard where the statue stood. It was much more than the site where I learned to roller-skate and engaged in marble games, or where I conducted my own New Years Eve fireworks exhibitions (something I cannot imagine happening for a child today in any town). It was much more.

The mustached sentinel was a symbol of pride—a constant. He never spoke a word, laughed, smiled, cried, or frowned. His stoic expression and stone-cold eyes were always resolute. He stood for heroic Confederate veterans whose names were etched below his lofty perch—heroic, at least, for part of the population. My great-grandfather's etching, Reverend John Martin Philip Otts, was earned by his service as a Chaplain at Fort Sumter when the war started and with the Greene County Confederate Reserves (Hale County not yet created) after coming to Greensboro during the war.

Dr. Otts was the first of the Otts line to bear the J. M. P. initials, often displayed after his ministerial title in lieu of the full name. While my father and my oldest brother were given the same name, there was no third due to the fact that my father's uncle was the original J. M. P. Junior, and died without a son. I have nothing against a family name being passed down as long as it does not carry some undue burden to replicate a dead person's life and accomplishments—expectations internalized but so often unrealized! My father and oldest brother may have carried some of that burden, perhaps exacerbated by the familial over-emphasis on storied ancestry.

Years before the Civil War, my great-great grandfather D. F. McCrary (father of my great-grandmother Lelia who married J. M. P.) came from a plantation family in North Carolina to establish his own fortunes in the boom area of Black Belt Alabama. Others also migrated due to the cotton-conducive black soil for which the Black Belt was named. It was a matter of cheap land due to the Indian Removal Act of 1830 and cheap labor in the form of slavery. Many small landowners also staked claims in those years. Fierce conflict and lasting resentment resulted from the federals overruling state provisions and seizing formerly Indian-owned land from settlers who had claimed it and moved their families there. Regardless of grass-roots growth, much of the economic and political power in Alabama belonged to the plantation barons, mostly concentrated in the Black Belt—dispro-portionately so in the area near Greensboro where three early governors made their homes.

The flat to mildly undulating land to the south of town is part of the rich black soil swath, but Greensboro proper is not. North of town, the terrain is hilly with a brown clay soil not nearly so conducive to agricultural fortune. Economically, my hometown has always been anchored in the rich Black Belt soil to its south. In antebellum times, some of the wealthy landowners lived on or near their prairie cotton plantations, but others like McCrary built estate homes in town with their primary cotton plantation holdings to the south.

My family was grounded in cotton as well as McCrary pride that was also nurtured through the merging lines of Lowry and Locke—back to the Earl of Granville and John Locke, the seventeenth-century English phi-losopher and physician. This heritage was instilled for many generations. In my time, it was not done so much by detailed stories as by rote ancestral pronouncements and references to symbols such as the stately Magnolia Hall built by D. F. McCrary in 1855. By this time, his cotton plantation to the south was very productive, and he also had established a lucrative business in town. Other valued symbols included paintings of ancestors, the inscribed Confederate statue, and historic, revered gravesites in a family plot appropriately marked by a magnolia tree that is still standing. In addition to the McCrary/Locke/Lowry heritage, my grandmother Jack's McEachin lineage formed still another ancestral aristocratic claim, this to Scotland and King Robert the Bruce. By the time I was old enough to pay attention, the entire family litany had been instilled repeatedly and in various ways.

The McCrarys had owned a sizable cotton plantation complete with many slaves until the end of the Civil War. In 1863, during the war, when Great-Grandfather Reverend J. M. P. Otts—of considerably more humble South Carolina beginnings—had migrated and married his beloved Lelia, she was the only surviving McCrary child, not that he married her for the fortune or ancestral glory. A number of preserved letters from J. M. P. to Lelia when they were apart speak eloquently of his affections. After several distant pastorates, the couple could not resist returning to an inherited Magnolia Hall upon her father's death in 1888.

The Otts continued to employ a number of former McCrary slaves, but fortunes began declining some time after the war. They received more of the inheritance when Lelia's mother died in 1901. Lelia and J. M. P. had nine sons, one of whom died in infancy. All eight survivors, including my grandfather Lee, were funded for success, and entered professions such as law and medicine. However, with the family inheritance divided among so many brothers and the Depression and cotton crash eating away at incomes—my family's substantive wealth in Greensboro continued to drop, and the boys were beginning to scatter away from the area.

Today, off Main Street about a mile east of the courthouse, Otts Street marks the way to the old mansion. With a rear facade that duplicates its six-pillared front, Magnolia Hall is on the National Register, and has received a lot of attention as a notable Greek Revival architectural structure. At the height of family fortune, grounds surrounding the home alone comprised much of what is now the residential area just east of downtown Greensboro. The bulk of family plantation property occupied many acres of Black Belt soil over twenty miles south near the village of Dayton.

Long before the demonstrations that 1965 summer, most of the McCrary/Otts property had been sold off. Only three lots remained under family ownership, including the largest Magnolia Hall property. One of the two others was deeded to my father by my grandmother. Her home was on the adjacent lot, both lots fronting Centreville Street. The larger Magnolia Hall property was separated from these by a corn field and another lot behind the Centreville Street properties.

As a boy, I got to Magnolia Hall by the cornfield route on foot and Main Street or a back street on bike. The property faced Main Street, and Otts Street began on what had been Reverend Otts's father-in-law McCrary's land. Today, it runs past other homes on some smaller lots, through the magnolia grove to a back street behind the house. A branching drive circles in front of the big house. Few in number and spread far and wide today, McCrary/Otts descendants no longer own any Greensboro property.

Even now, the smell of blooming magnolias takes my mind back to childhood journeys through the magnificent old magnolia trees in the grove surrounding Magnolia Hall and up into their huge, accommodating limbs. There, I fell into childhood fantasies, mostly adventurous ones that involved military heroism and confronting the invading enemy in defense of Magnolia Hall. In the delirium of magnolia blossoms, I defended honor and pride against the Northerners. While not nearly so dramatic as Scarlett O'Hara's obsession with Tara, something within me was compellingly attached to that place—at least in the best years of my creative thinking as a youth.

My grandfather, one of the eight brothers surviving to adulthood, stayed in Greensboro and died well before I was born. His widow, Eudora, my grandmother of McEachin stock based in Tuscaloosa, was an interesting character. She lived next door to us in the relatively modest four-columned antebellum house where my father was born. It was built on McCrary land by D. F.'s brother, and later purchased from him by his nephew, my grandfather, Lee M. Otts. After Lee's death, my grandmother continued to live there. Her daughter and hard-working son-in-law, along with their three children—all older than me—lived with her.

My grandmother, totally blind when she reached her eighties as I remember her, not only cussed a blue streak but was about as hard-headed as anyone could be. She insisted that everyone call her Jack, a childhood nickname. Everyone did, or else! Nobody knew what the *or else* entailed because nobody dared find out. When I was a boy, our Alabama family members from near and far gathered at my grandmother's house every Christmas Eve, a type of reunion event. This high-spirited gathering took place in a large high-ceiling parlor, overseen by painted ancestors and in front of an enormous Christmas tree. Adults seated in chairs and youngsters on the floor, we would take turns opening presents.

My grandmother made an obligation one Christmas Eve that became an annual tradition by announcing that she would try on any gift of clothing right on the spot. To the kids' delight, she received a pair of panties one Christmas Eve. In front of our crowd of maybe thirty or forty, my eighty-something-year-old blind grandmother struggled to her feet and put those panties on under her dress. We youngsters howled and rolled to no end! She was a character and a pure hoot when she fancied it.

Jack was an oft-complaining loud matriarch in her later years, but she had a soft side not often revealed. When I was still in elementary school, she would frequently call me over to her house to sit in a chair in her large bedroom, also used as a sitting room with windows facing the front porch and yard. There, relaxing in her well-worn and overstuffed chair, my blind grandmother would ask me to describe the front yard scene visible through the windows.

I was not confident at first, but finding the crusty lady to be nonjudg-mental and appreciative, I eventually took to the ritual with enthusiasm. She would often urge me to continue the color commentary even when I was ready to stop. I learned how to describe individual squirrels and birds, wind-prompted movement of leaves on the old oak trees, and variations of color in the many camellia blooms in season. She took delight in it and remarked once that it was almost like seeing again. It helped me in terms of both communication and appreciation for nature, and I like to think that my grandmother knew it was good for me.

Beyond ancestral reinforcements, I was certainly put on notice as to my status relative to others—particularly black others—at an early age. Not everyone has had that message delivered so succinctly as in Jack's whispered *better than them* pronouncement, though many have received it one way or another. I think there is a belief, more prevalent in some cultures than others, that finding a way to elevate yourself relative to those around you provides a solid form of self-esteem. In that context, my grandmother thought she was giving me something important.

One of the town's eccentrics was my great-aunt by marriage. Upon my great-grandmother's death, Magnolia Hall was acquired by one of her sons, J. W. , a photographer whose work is seen in one image herein. He married this eccentric woman also of notable lineage, a Randolph of the Virginia Randolphs. When J. W. died, Aunt Sadie became the red-haired, tall-and-skinny fear of my life. She lived in that old mansion with her sister who came from Virginia and did not leave. The sister was considerably shorter than Aunt Sadie, and her hair was a lighter red. Aunt Sadie's dyed hair was downright fiery, even in her advanced years. The widow and her spinster sister made an interesting Mutt and Jeff pair, but Aunt Sadie put her sister in the shade when it came to being eccentric.

Rarely would I be detected in the magnolia grove when acting out my dreams, for Aunt Sadie and sister rarely emerged from their stately residence except in some very predictable routines I committed to memory—out of necessity! Aunt Sadie was fond of wearing a fox stole, the type with a shrunken fox head that bit the tail, serving as the clasp for the stole. That itself would not be so strange: fox stoles were fashionable among certain women of the time. But Aunt Sadie wore hers in the heat of summer,and that stole combined with Aunt Sadie's other eccentricities was too much for me! The dead fox froze this little boy with fear whenever the red-haired lady approached. I had one simple strategy—run! In the regretful event that my mother was present, I was restrained to await the dreaded moment. Aunt Sadie would lean over with hair coming down like a fireball—bright red lipstick and false teeth glistening, the dead fox descending like a hound from hell! Even if I avoided the beady-eyed fox head, I would still receive a bright red lipstick smear upon my contorted lips—if her aim was good.

In college, I was told repeatedly on visits home that I should drop by Magnolia Hall to visit my eccentric aunt. In a state of declining health, she would likely die soon, and wanted to leave the old house to someone on our side of the family, or so they said. Unfortunately, Aunt Sadie did not consider anyone worthy, save possibly—you guessed it—the boy who could not avoid all of her dead fox kisses. By then, there was no longer anything compelling to me about Magnolia Hall, no mystique. With no intention of moving back to Greensboro, I was quite headstrong about the matter, and refused to comply. The old house would cost a fortune to be restored anyway. On hindsight, considering what happened subsequently, I guess I would have acted differently

The long and short of Magnolia Hall and Aunt Sadie is that after she died, her sister, as the closest relative and in absence of a will, inherited the house. This was an outrage to the Otts family and a boon to the sister. By the time of her death, Aunt Sadie had very little money for anyone to inherit, but like a scene from a Gothic novel, the little sister found some old stock certificates jammed in an upstairs wardrobe in that old house. The discovery made her independently wealthy. The sister got a load of money, but did not possess it for long. Around a year afterwards, she also died. The Randolph family, through their affiliation with the Episcopal Church, put the house up for bid in what turned out to be a controversial process. I was told that a bid from someone in our family was not received within the time limit, and there was much controversy about the nature of the limit itself.

A compromise was arranged by the attorney in charge so that family members received some treasured furnishings and backed away from potential legal action, having low odds for success. Seeing Magnolia Hall slip away from the family was indeed a blow to what was left of the ancient pride. Fortunately, the bid winners lived there for a long time and did their best with the house and property. As of this writing, it has been secured by someone having a tremendous interest in historical preservation and has been restored to its antebellum best. Our relatives may drive by Magnolia Hall occasionally today, but the power of lineage and pride it once represented has dwindled considerably. Perhaps that is also deserving of restoration, in an adjusted form. I have wondered if my attitudes toward others, in terms of skin color or otherwise, might have been any different if I had not rejected the supposed opportunity to own Magnolia Hall. Treasures of this type can be powerful.

9

SLAVERY AND THE SLAVE BALCONY

A labama's original 1819 state constitution was a progressive human rights document. It gave the vote to white male citizens without property, tax payment, or militia service requirements. It also gave all who were eligible to vote the opportunity to seek public office. At that time, Kentucky's was the only other state constitution offering such provisions. Even more remarkable, though slavery was sanctioned as in all states, Alabama's constitution actually provided that slaves were to be treated *with humanity*, to be provided with necessary food and clothing, and that slaveholders were to "abstain from all injuries to them extending to life and limb."

If a slaveholder killed a slave, his punishment was to be the same as it would be if the victim was a "free white person" (excepting killings during an insurrection). Two of Alabama's original constitution drafters and later governors unsuccessfully tried to give their legislatures the power to extend voting rights to free blacks.

Given its progressive beginnings with voting rights and treatment of slaves, why didn't Alabama eventually eliminate slavery as many states did through court rulings and legislative changes? One factor is that contents of the original constitution did not have to be ratified by voters so nobody knew the values of the voting public on these matters. Still, Alabama's lack of subsequent progress may have related more to machine than politics, though much did later become institutionalized in law. Eli Whitney's 1793 invention of the cotton gin made the production of cotton more efficient and profitable. This led to a greater need for labor to harvest, and slaves presented a cheap answer to that need. I'm not saying that the gin or cotton alone caused slavery, but I do believe it could have been more easily remedied if cotton was not so integral to overall economic fortune.

Cotton was truly king in the early to mid nineteenth century. Consider the words of a British visitor as recorded in *Belle Brittan on a Tour, at Newport, and Here and There* by Hiram Fuller (published by Derby & Jackson in 1858). He said the port city of Mobile was "where the people live in cotton houses and ride in cotton carriages. They buy cotton, sell cotton, think cotton, eat cotton, drink cotton, and dream cotton. They marry cotton wives, and unto them are born cotton children . . . It is the great staple—the sum and substance of Alabama. It has made Mobile and all its citizens."

King Cotton ascended through slave trading—witness comments from a Yankee visitor to Alabama in 1835 who said, "To sell cotton in order to buy negroes—to make more cotton to buy more negroes, ad infinitum, is the aim and direct tendency of all the operations of the thorough-going planter. . . . his whole soul is wrapped up in the pursuit." This penetrating quote comes from *The Americans: The National Experience* by Daniel Boorstin (Random House, 1965).

It is much easier for me to understand the scope of slavery as perpetuated by profit motives than simply by human desires to dominate and wreak misery upon others—though it would require a denial of mankind's history to think sheer cruelty played no part at all for at least some slaveowners. I do believe that the drive to elevate self at the expense of others was probably a reinforcing psychological factor to different individual degrees—futile attempts to meet unmet self-esteem needs similar to those I had that day on the curb almost a century later.

Slavery was institutionalized in many ways peculiar to the South. Consider the summary given by Christine Heyrman in *Southern Cross: The Beginnings of the Bible Belt*: "Baptists and Methodists rose steadily to defend slavery in the 1830s, secession in the 1850s, and the holy cause of upholding both with force in 1861. . . ."

Not all, but many white preachers in different churches were spouting their justifying commentaries out of context, as would be the case over segregation a century later. Exceptions usually drew heat.

In the days of slavery reinforcement by churches, some very interesting dependencies were at work. Edward Crowther wrote a 1992 *Journal of Southern History* article, "Holy Honor: Sacred and Secular in the Old South." He posited that the planter and the preacher had a symbiotic relationship. The planter needed a "moral defense" of his intertwined roles as functional father, husband, and slave master. He needed the preacher as an authoritative source to reconcile the contrasts or to justify himself morally. As for the preacher, he needed the planter's stamp of approval as a man of status and influence in the community and congregation. Common sense says that the planter being a major church donor was another element in this symbiotic relationship.

Of course, the dependent nature of such relationships was not so much the case for other whites living off the sweat of their brows day to day. However, the influence was visited on them as church members or as members of the community. In the heat of conflict, some—again, not all—ministers referenced Northerners as atheists, socialists, or anti-Christian people. As *Watchman* editor Cobbs stated in one of his editorials, "It was a small wonder that in the wake of the war, when asked who had crucified Christ, a young southern girl responded immediately, 'O, yes, I know … they Yankees.'"

The Greensboro Presbyterian Church at the corner of Main and Demopolis streets is visible from the site where marchers were arrested and bused to Selma. Organized in 1823, and my great-grandfather's first pastorate almost forty years later, the church building is now considered one of the historic sites of Greensboro. On Sundays, we always sat in the Otts pew (when I was a child, it was not officially reserved for us but generally understood to be ours). The sanctuary's beautiful, tall, ornate, stained-glass windows are still magnificent, depicting various scenes in the life of Jesus. Names and years of service for various past pastors and other congregational leaders are emblazoned upon the lower, outward-opening sections of the windows. Reverend J. M. P. Otts and wife Lelia are memorialized on two, one directly across the outside aisle from the Otts pew.

Many visitors to Greensboro check out this historic building with its red brick exterior and tall steeple rising from a shingled roof. The ornate windows, massive wooden pulpit, golden organ pipes, and high wood-beamed ceiling are impressive. At the back of the sanctuary, clearly visible only by peering up from near the pulpit at the front, there is a dark balcony area.

Each time I returned to the old church, always for funeral services, that balcony seemed darker. I do not think anyone occupies it much during services today, same as in my youth.

The state historical marker fronting the church building contains information on the original 1823 building, its original founders and this: "Original wooden structure replaced by brick building in 1841. . . . Present building erected in 1859 when Rev. J. C. Mitchell was pastor. Old slave gallery may still be seen." The gallery was the balcony. According to a "Historical Sermon" recorded in the July 6, 1883, edition of the New Orleans publication *South-Western Presbyterian*, a statistical report of the Greensboro Presbyterian Church was provided from the pulpit in 1861—just before J. M. P. assumed the pastorate in 1862. There were eighty members, twenty of whom were "colored." Everything I gathered shows that Rev. Otts presided over a racially mixed flock even after the Civil War ended, up to his assumption of another church pulpit in 1867. He was a spiritual scholar, and his sermons must have been moving to the gentry, including those plantation owners among whom was D. F. McCrary, his wife Elizabeth, and daughter Lelia, by that time a winsome teenager. The hand fans surely fluttered those hot summer Sundays as the reverend presided over his white floor-level flock in that magnificent sanctuary.

I wonder how much warmer it might have been for the others who were watching and listening from their lofty but lowly perches on unpadded pews above. On visiting the church building recently and standing behind the pulpit, it occurred to me that he must have occasionally looked up and gazed into their dark eyes hungering for hope. He was there to give just that. Yet, as the crowd filed out after services through the large front doors, those balcony-dwellers were not to be seen—not to shake his hand or congratulate him on a well-prepared message. Instead, they would have been in their "rightful place," descending from the balcony in a narrow dark stairwell and filing out of a separate exit. When considering this, my only way to even remotely fathom it was to remember the day I held that tire iron so tight. Still, standing behind that pulpit, I was perplexed.

After slavery ended, historical records indicate that some free blacks remained in attendance. *Historical Notes on the Greensboro Presbyterian*

Church—as recorded for the congregation by Lutie James Davidson in 1959—indicates that the minister, Dr. Clark, wrote in his notes that "prior to 1844 there were received into the church about 220 white persons and a large number of colored persons, the latter at some dates equaling the number of white communicants." Davidson also reported that "the gallery still in the building was occupied during services by the slaves. They joined in the hymns. On Communion Sundays after the white congregation was served, they were invited down to sit on the left front pews, where they were also served Communion. This applied even after they were freed as long as they were present."

As part of new construction in 1859, this "gallery" or balcony was made for slaves. They deserved that much, if not for their eternal worth, for back-breaking work in the cotton fields, for raising the master's children, for cooking the meals, or for doing all manner of manual tasks. However, it is possible that building a slave balcony or developing some other separate seating for slaves in a church was based on some less noble motivations. An 1852 Alabama law required whites to be present during all religious services attended by blacks. This law clearly demonstrated white fears of black religious gatherings—or gatherings of any sort. Over twenty years earlier, there was a Virginia slave rebellion led by Nat Turner in which a number of whites were killed. While not concluding anything about motivations in this particular congregation without more information, it's not far-fetched to speculate that slave balconies or other separate provisions in church buildings could have been a convenient way to obey the law and quell fears.

Slavery was inherently cruel, but I do not believe that all slaveholders were necessarily cruel in the way they treated slaves. In keeping with the fear factor, the law made it illegal to teach slaves to read or write. Many whites ignored that, and some were slaveholders who taught slaves to read the Bible for themselves. It seems if they simply wanted slaves pacified by religion, they would teach and quote the Bible selectively to that end. Why teach them to read it for themselves? In fairness, and again without more to form a firm conclusion, I decided that this particular slave balcony could have been constructed from noble or ignoble motivations—or from both!

Regardless of the kind natures of some slaveholders and some laws of relatively humane treatment, a number of whites and slaveholders did cruel things to slaves. Though there were laws prohibiting selling slave children apart from their families, it was done at times. At one time, in Alabama, rape of a black woman by either a black man or a white master was not even considered a crime. While I have no reason to think that white masters having sex with their female slaves was standard practice, I have no doubt it occurred at times, not making a call on how much.

According to *Alabama: The History of a Deep South State* (University of Alabama Press, 1994), an Alabama governor's wife was mortified to learn that a slave owner's child and his son's child were their slaves. She even heard that both children may have had the same slave mother—as a result of being impregnated by both the slave owner and his son. At the same time, some free blacks in Alabama were slaveholders. Talk about perplexing!

Even considering my own attitude in 1965, it is difficult to understand how any good people could condone a system of slavery when it is so undeniably evil. History is full of injustice and cruelty, including abject horrors such as the Holocaust. However, something else that was undeniable about those times of slavery was well stated, again in *The History of a Deep South State*: "The irony of it was that so many humans, black and white, were able to live out their lives with honor and dignity within such a society."

Davidson's church history goes on to portray the development of a black church composed of former members of the Greensboro Presbyterian Church: "The Minutes of the Session September 1, 1884, stated that these colored communicants were dismissed to organize the Joppa Church—Algernon Duval, Dorcas Duval, John Robinson, Henry P. Thurman, P. J. Keith, Charity Keith, William G. Field. Samuel Locke was also a member of Joppa." It struck me that my lauded family heritage includes the prestigious Locke line through my great-great grandmother.

John Locke was a relative of my great-great grandmother, Elizabeth Cowan McCrary. He was a slaveholder in the area appointed to be an elder at the Greensboro Presbyterian Church in 1840 at the same time as Elizabeth's husband, D. F. McCrary, my great-great grandfather. Considering the rarity of the surname, the church commonality, and the timing, Samuel Locke could well have carried the Locke name through his or his family's bondage to my ancestors—not a rare practice.

The same reference to Session minutes states that there was an application attached for a loan to form the Joppa church. Davidson wrote that, subsequently, the new congregation's numbers eventually diminished to the point of dissolution. I cannot say for certain whose motivations were central to this new church formation, nor do I know the nature of those motivations. After slave members gained freedom and as their children matured, I can easily understand and appreciate that black members might be motivated to form separate black churches. Nothing tells me there was any pressure for them to leave, but that is a possibility as well. Beyond motivations, something else gave me pause for thought about this separation. Since some black people remained members of predominantly white churches for some time after emancipation (in this case, almost twenty years), and given that there are so many segregated church assemblies today, was a potential source of future social integration lost with those church formations?

10

Anonymous People, Mammy's Passing, Booker T., and JMP

The port city of Mobile was a hub of imported slave traffic, and records indicate that Great-great grandfather McCrary was on the receiving end for many of those slaves. In fact, he was among the area plantation owners who had the most. The image of slaves as typically *contented darkies* was not accurate at all, no matter what some people wanted to justify then or to romanticize historically now. On the other hand, there were caring relationships between some slaves and masters, no matter how broadly some people have wanted to paint the cruelty of slavery then or now. The following obituary appeared in the *Greensboro Watchman*, dated December 3, 1891.

> Becky Butts, colored, who had been a servant in the family of the late Mr. D. F. McCrary for 67 years, died last Sunday night, on Dr. J. M. P. Otts' place in Greensboro, aged about 80 years. She is spoken of in the highest terms by those whom she had served so long and faithfully.

Such an obituary for *a servant* is about as touching as it could possibly be in those times. Butts was obviously a slave with the McCrarys, and continued as a worker in the Otts household post-emancipation. Backdating from her obituary, she would have been counted as a slave in service to the McCrary family at age thirteen in 1824—prior to D. F. McCrary's migration from North Carolina, estimated as some time in the 1830s. Our family history does indicate that some trusted slaves migrated with him. Becky Butts was only a year older than D. F., and both would probably have been in their twenties when the move to Alabama took place. Due to her age and other factors, I believe Becky Butts was probably the same person as a known slave for the McCrary family, Miss Spicey McCrary—name being consistent with the practice of referencing slaves by slaveholder surname and nicknames given by slaveholders. It's understandable, maybe even expected, that someone in slavery or his or her descendants would discontinue using the slaveholder's name or nickname after the abolition of slavery—that and perhaps marriage accounting for the name difference between Spicey McCrary and Becky Butts.

One reference to Spicey occurred in a letter responding to genealogical inquiry from one of my grandfather's brothers in the early 1930s. His cousin, Annie Locke—then residing in Dayton, Alabama—said that Miss Spicey had been very devoted to Mrs. Elizabeth Cowan McCrary (Betty) and to her daughter, Lelia Jane McCrary, who married my great-grandfather to become Mrs. J. M. P. Otts. Locke quoted Miss Spicey as saying, "Miss Betty glorified in her own kin, and Miss Lelia is just like her." This statement could mean devoted to current family, but it would be consistent with traditional family emphasis (as well as the context of Locke's response to an inquiry about genealogy) to conclude that Miss Spicey more likely was referring to the pride Elizabeth (Betty) McCrary and daughter Lelia took in their ancestry through the lines of Locke and Lowry.

My search of records to prove my presumption that Becky Butts and Spicey McCrary were the same person was fruitless, and I became very frustrated. Finally, encountering what I would call an anonymity factor related to names in slavery and changes, I gave up. The magnitude and generational implications of slavery begs the ancestry question in a uniquely intense way, for at least some black people, even today. Failing to gain any knowledge of what happened to their ancestors has to produce a much higher sense of frustration than what I experienced.

On a more speculative but compelling level for me, evidence also suggested that Becky/Spicey could have been the so-called *nanny* for McCrary's only surviving daughter, my Great-grandmother Lelia. Such a relationship would be consistent with the storied scenario of some plantation owners' wives assigning childcare responsibility to trusted slave women. In the context of dark times for the McCrarys, it would have been even more needed than normal. For simplicity, I'll refer to the woman only as Becky.

She would have been around thirty-eight when Lelia was born. The relationship between a nanny and Lelia could have been so needed—and even deepened—due to the fact that Lelia was a firstborn (of two children) who became an only surviving child at age three when her little sister died of a malady unknown to us. Georgeanna was just over a year old when she died. No doubt, their mother, Elizabeth (called Betty) would have needed experienced, trusted help, and the circumstances would promote a long relationship in that regard. The older Becky would have been a natural choice, and it would certainly explain her longevity in family service—her bond with Lelia leading to the sensitive obituary upon her death. Still, with nothing more to go on, I gave my speculation only passing consideration until I came upon the old song, "The Passing of Mammy." That was when the speculation became compelling.

In the course of research, I was referred to an old book, *Plantation Songs for My Lady's Banjo*, with illustrative photos by J. W. Otts, one of my grandfather's eight brothers I never knew. He brought his photography business from Marion back to Greensboro to live with his mother, Lelia, at Magnolia Hall upon his father J. M. P.'s death. J. W. subsequently married my eccentric Great-aunt Sadie and they lived at Magnolia Hall through his mother's death and until his death left Sadie alone there. Doubtless, J. W. would have known Becky Butts well as his mother's presumed former nanny and obviously valued companion in later years per Becky's obituary.

Plantation Songs for My Lady's Banjo by Eli Shepperd was originally published in 1901 and re-published in 1977 by Sergeant Kirkland's Museum and Historical Society, Inc., Fredericksburg, Virginia. Eli Shepperd was a pen name for Martha Young who published other books and was born near Greensboro in 1868. It seems that Young felt she needed a pen name in a man's world of authors at the time. She grew up during reconstruction, never married, and lived in Greensboro as an adult when writing for publication. I discovered that her home at that time was what I knew as the old Perry house on Centreville Street. It was located on the other side of my grandmother's home, two doors down from us. It was familiar to me as the place where Miss Martin, my inspiring high school literature teacher, lived in an apartment in the 1960s.

Before reading the book, I thumbed through J. W.'s photographs, finding that several matched their narratives in sensitive, evocative ways. As Young's photographer for the book, J. W. Otts used Magnolia Hall (where he lived at the time) as a very appropriate backdrop for some key photographs. In the reading, I found myself captivated by oral songs and poetry, stories told by some downtrodden and yet amazingly positive people who had been slaves. Good portrayals of plantation life and expression included the moving "The Passing of Mammy," along with its accompanying photograph of a black woman holding a white baby. The poem and photograph gave me so much more to consider about the potential role of Becky Butts in my ancestral family and about the role other trusted women may have played for other white plantation owners' children across the South.

Regardless of the sensitivities some may have about the use of dialect in literature, I was appreciative for the original language used throughout the book. It was so alive and emotionally rich. I thought about providing only a portion of "The Passing of Mammy" here, but could not shortchange your experience of its range—so much said in so few words. The first four lines set the scene.

Ah, there in the dusky cabin,
With the smouldering "chunks" on the hearth,
Reached the dark old arms that had clasped her,
Loved, tended, and held her from birth.
"You, Babsey, — you l'il' gal! You Petsey!
You is done come to Mam' Jo!
De niggers all say you wouldn't,
I tole 'em you would: Des so!
Di'n't you useter leave yo' Ma
When I'd call you to come? — ho-ho!
Dat useter make Mistis mos' cry
To see how you'd come when I'd call —
I do b'lieve de chile love you, Jo,
Mo' 'me and her Pa, and all!'
Oh, Honey, de ole times is banished,

Gone whar de ole times go,
Us don't know whar dey be vanished,
Des know dey don't come no mo'.
You sorry I lef you all, li'l' Miss?
Well — I gwine lef dem all now —
Co's Rosser was des a nigger,
But den he was mine, anyhow.
Dis cough — No'm — No doctor — No money —
But don't you fret 'bout dat, chile,
God's will cyarn't be stopped no way, Honey,
And us all bound to go somewhile.
I sont fer you now, lit Lady
(I done miss you so all dese years),
Fer to ax you to meet me in Glory,—
I gwine miss you dar, too, I fears,
Dis black preacher heah to Swamp Church
He says no white pusson cyarn't go
Nairy bit way furder in Heaven
Dan de ve'y outermos' do'.
But I'm gwine ax de Good Master
To — 'Please, Sah !' — des let you in!
'Case I don't wanter go 'long feruvver
Missin' you so ag'in.
I know you cyarn't have much 'ligion
'Caze you ain't never had no chance,
But de Lord won't be hard on you, Honey,
When I tell him des way things advance —
You al'a's had so much er money,
And no trouble to draw you nigh
(Who ? — my ole Massa's Gran'chile;
Troubles 'bleeged to pass her by!),
And you al'a's had gracious plenty
Of mighty good things to eat.
Naw, you don't know how quick, my darlin',

Honger'll drop you right down to God's feet.
Some mornin's when I does so miss
My sugar and coffee or tea,
I hatter wrestle in prayer some hours
'Fo' my stomach and soul'll agree—
Oh yas—yas—Honey! Byelo-o-o—
Singing
"You li'l' Lady, bye,—lo-bye—
Shet yo' li'l' sleepy eye,
Mammy gwine fetch you a dream by-m-by—
Way fum de moon dat float so high.
Mammy gwine fetch you a nice li'l' dream—
De way things are and de way dey seem—
Bye, my pretty li'l' baby, you,
Sleepin sof'ly now, fer true—
Hush—'sh—'s-h-h—
"Eh? Whar was I? I thought I was gone—
Sho' my ears caught de plenteous sound,
De rollin' of Jorden's deep waters,
Cross which my soul is bound—
Nummine, my Honey, yo' Mammy'll
Wait fer you right clost to de Gate—
She'll stay dar waitin', li'l' Missy,
Nummine ef hit do be late.
And I'll ax de Good Lord: 'Please, Sah! Massa!
Des give my li'l' Missy a seat,
And some nice li'l' gol'en slippers,'—
Fit yo' neat li'l' feet ;
And a gol'en crown fer you, Lady !
Ef I ax him he'll fix you up right—
Dough you is—Mammy's lil' Lady—
Dough you is—only—des white."

Mammy's loving depth of emotion is something anyone should be able to appreciate—a bond that transcends the bondage of slavery. We are all the same inside, at the level of human need and emotions, in the depth of our hearts. Love is not enslaved by skin color. While I'm not sure about "Petsey," "Babsey" was sometimes a way of referring affectionately to a baby or younger child. Chances are the person visiting Mammy was no longer a child, but still her *baby* as is commonly the case with children you raised or helped raise. Of course, Becky died ten years before the book was published, but that does not rule her out as the inspiration for the poem. Lelia was certainly born with the proverbial silver spoon in her mouth, and that matches the poignant narrative. In fact, everywhere I turned in researching this led me right back to Becky and Lelia—and a passing consideration slowly became a very good possibility.

Given the location, timing, and J. W.'s role, I thought it logical that the child posed for the photograph could have been one of my grandparents' four children. Their grandparents would have been J. M. P. and Lelia. Since J. W. Otts and Martha Young were both childless, it added to the logic. Also, Martha Young lived right next door to my grandparents and their young children, including my father, his brother, and two sisters. Various factors considered, including the presumption the child posed was a girl and her likely age, led me and my family-knowledgable nephew to conclude that the most likely candidate was their daughter, my aunt Lelia—named after her grandmother.

At first, it appeared that my loosely held theory of the poem being modeled after the relationship between Becky and Lelia might be discounted since the ending of the poem seems to indicate the child was the granddaughter (not the child) of Mammy's *ole Massa*. Lelia would have been the child of D. F. McCrary, not his grandchild. However, more research led me to conclude that the old master reference could well have been directed to Becky's oldest master and plantation owner in North Carolina before she came down with his son D. F.'s entourage in her twenties, having been a slave for the elder McCrary for years—truly the *ole Massa*. He would have been Lelia's grandfather, and I found some irresistible logic as well in the fact that the McCrary fortune, object of Mammy's reference, was nurtured by the elder one, and the Alabama McCrary branch had likely not known hard times in this regard. My projection of Becky as Spicey was fairly solid and as a probable Mammy figure for Lelia, less solid but still strong for a number of reasons. The projection that the model for the photograph was Aunt Lelia was intriguing and not far-fetched. All I had were speculations, especially since research was hindered by the manner in which slave identities were vague in the record. How many have longed to complete a family puzzle by talking with ancestors? More perplexing is to consider how many have faced daunting—even haunting—speculations when their ancestors were slaves made anonymous by their status.

For me, Becky could only be imagined, and so I imagined her. I imagined Becky as Miss Spicey, a young woman in slavery making the long trip down to Alabama with other slaves (possibly with parents and siblings), D. F. McCrary, and possibly his brother since he also had holdings in the Greensboro area. This would be consistent with a D. F. McCrary slave census that included ages but not identities. I imagined Becky's involvement in wedding preparations for D. F. and Elizabeth (*Miss Betty*), helping with the birth of Lelia as their first child, and sharing their grief in the loss of their second, little Georgeanna. I imagined her caretaker's role with three-year-old Lelia increasing during the baby's illness, followed by an extended time of parental mourning after death. This and the caring service Becky extended throughout Lelia's lifetime would produce the strong bond as described by the poem/song and Becky's loving obituary—by all accounts, probably composed by Lelia herself. I imagined Becky as Mammy in declining health and pouring out her heart to her *Babsey* whom she loved so much.

While you can't apply blanket profiles to all slaves and owners, I think this monologue song says something meaningfully ironic about the difference between many slaves and their owners when it came to faith. For many slaves, as portrayed in "The Passing of Mammy," their spirituality flourished even in the midst of their bondage. They had to appreciate sentiments like those expressed by the *preacher heah to Swamp Church* and Biblical parables like the Rich Young Ruler wherein Jesus compared a rich person's prospects of entering the kingdom of heaven to that of a camel passing through the eye of a needle.

While not all slaveholders were rich, it does seem reasonable to think some, perhaps many, wealthy plantation owners could not easily recognize their own deepest needs or shortcomings with truly humble hearts, a form of spiritual depravity. When people view themselves as inherently better than others, it seems they are somewhat bound to that form of depravity—a form of slavery as Martin Luther King saw it. So it was for me. Whether in 1865, 1965, or today, some people who are bigoted toward an entire race of people can still be good people in other ways, good but unable or unwilling to face their conflicts. I think psychologists might call much of this *compartmentalizing*, a process through which people can avoid seeing conflicts between different areas of their lives by mentally keeping them in isolated boxes. It's not psycho-babble. Most of us do this to varying degrees at one time or another with issues in our lives.

Lelia's husband, my great-grandfather, Reverend J. M. P. Otts, obtained his doctorate of divinity from Davidson College in South Carolina. Some years later, he endowed a chair at Davidson, where lectureships continue today as the Otts Lecture Series. As a chaplain in the Confederate Army, he served at the fall of Fort Sumter. Rev. Otts's early discharge and assumption of a pastorate at the First Presbyterian Church of Greensboro resulted from a now-unknown illness that called for a milder climate.

Much more happened to Reverend Otts than getting his name inscribed on a statue. Not a silver-spoon child at all, he was born to two parents who were both rural teachers—an unlikely candidate for the hand of the lovely, precocious, and wealthy Lelia Jane McCrary. However, just under two years after arriving in Greensboro as pastor of the McCrarys' church congregation, J. M. P. married Lelia. After nurturing the Greensboro Presbyterian Church for several years, Rev. Otts advanced to other locations, the most impressive being the pastorate at Chambers Presbyterian Church in Philadelphia, Pennsylvania, supposedly the largest Presbyterian Church in the U.S. at the time. He was dubbed by President Harding as a special emissary to France and traveled internationally while retaining pastoral duties. Otts was a widely published author of Christian-themed books, including a study of the French Huguenots, an expose on Jerusalem, as well as books about Biblical gospel accounts.

In 1887, Alabama Governor Thomas Seay (one of the Alabama governors from the Greensboro area) appointed Reverend Otts to the board of trustees of the Alabama Colored People's University. He served as the Board's first president during an important period in the history of predominantly black Alabama institutions of higher learning. Early in his tenure, he was involved in consideration of a potential merger of the University with Tuskegee Institute. An intriguing letter from E. J. Carter to Tuskegee Principal Booker T. Washington was dated July 3, 1887, and is published in the Booker T. Washington Papers collection at Illinois University.

Dear Friend,

I received your letter a few days ago, and noted the contents. Dr. Otts was away when I received yours but returned day before yesterday evening. I went to see him yesterday morning and had a long talk with him about the location of the university. I have done what I could against Montgomery for your sake, and for the sake of the race. Do you know that the white people are thinking about uniting your school with the other university? If you don't know it, I will tell you they are and they intend to make Mr. Patterson the Principal. The governor is not allowing the Negro the chance of a dog in this matter, but let us work and wait. I hope you will be as unmovable as the everlasting mountain. Both Republican and democrat are trying to keep the Negro behind them, but God is leading on the army and if we will be led by him he will "carry us through". You have done a good work since you have come to Ala., and have thus planted yourself Imperishably in the hearts of your people. You have my prayers and my influence for the success of your good work. I believe you will succeed, for I know God is on your side.

Your Friend, E. J. Carter

Booker T. Washington was born in slavery on a small plantation in Virginia. After the Civil War, he graduated from Hampton Institute and then became the principal of Tuskegee Institute. Of course, as the letter indicates, maintaining control of the Institute was a political challenge with racial overtones. The letter does not directly assert anything about my great-grandfather's position on the merger issue, but I take it that he may have at least been informative for Mr. Washington's purposes. The Institute remained intact, and it has served as an important steppingstone for many young black men and women over the years.

The Alabama Colored People's University was relocated to Montgomery, went through some name changes, and is now known as Alabama State University—also a prestigious institution and launching pad for great accomplishments by so many over the years. As for my great grandfather's tenure as board president, I did not know about it until doing research for this book. Given a strong family tendency to bask in ancestors' accomplishments and promote better-than-them thinking in regard to black people, my ignorance about that important role just might be attributed to family avoidance—or maybe even denial. I came to view J. M. P.'s work in regard to higher education for black people as a type of balm, and like to think perhaps he did see and could not forget those faces in the balcony.

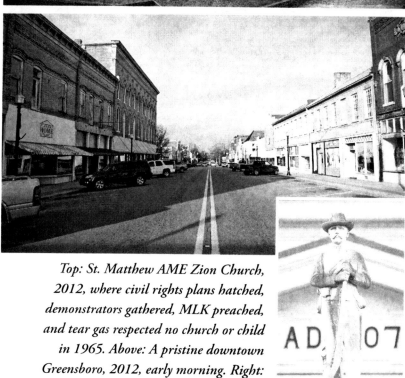

Top: St. Matthew AME Zion Church, 2012, where civil rights plans hatched, demonstrators gathered, MLK preached, and tear gas respected no church or child in 1965. Above: A pristine downtown Greensboro, 2012, early morning. Right: A resolute but worn sentinel, 2012. (All by Zach Riggins Photography)

Right: Courthouse and statue, 2012, as seen from near author's 1965 vantage point. Below: Through an aged fence, courthouse clock tower looms over abandoned jail, 2012— eerily the same. (Zach Riggins Photography)

Above: Safe House Museum, 2012— visitors will walk alongside surreal images of '60s marchers.
Left: Genuine KKK robe in a Safe House Museum display, 2012.
(Zach Riggins Photography)

Greensboro Presbyterian Church sanctuary as seen from former slave balcony, 2012. (Zach Riggins Photography)

Treasured Magnolia Hall, 2012—front and back views.
(Zach Riggins Photography)

J. W. Otts's depiction of Plantation Songs "Mammy" as a household slave holding plantation owner's white child, mid-19th century, and family photo of grandmother's household help holding author's sister at her birthday party a century later.

Left: A younger Great Aunt Sadie and the feared fox. Below: Sarah, a gentle spirit and great influence.

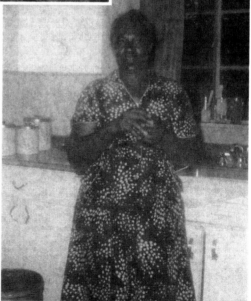

Top: *Demonstrators at the barricade, summer of 1965—Theresa Burroughs is notable here and in other important demonstrations across Alabama. Bottom: A brave and defiant Alice Hargress and friend under arrest, summer of 1965. (Alabama Department of Public Safety)*

11

For Where Your Treasure Is . . .

ride in ancestry can be constructive. However, if pride can't stand on its own without lowering others, it is actually dependent. I never knew either of my grandfathers. According to my mother, my paternal grandfather—a good man in her estimation—was broken by the Great Depression and perhaps died before his time due to the pressure of financial ruin. He was a practicing attorney and local bank president when all became bleak, actually escaping the worst by being appointed local postmaster through family connections in Washington. Still, like many in the throes of that economic crisis, he suffered severe damage to his pride. It wreaked unspeakable havoc upon many with little to live on, but the internal blow delivered to the rich and proud could also be devastating.

After her husband's death, my grandmother Jack and the attached family in Greensboro continued down a slippery financial slope. It didn't help that alcohol was central for many family members, and it seems the family lineage took on even more significance, perhaps a crutch for some. My father stopped drinking when I was twelve. I heard it was because a doctor told him he would die otherwise, but I don't know for sure. In time, he actually helped others struggling with a drinking problem. His younger sister also had alcohol problems. His older sister Lelia, presumably the *Babsey* model, became the wife of an Alabama attorney general and was also possessed by alcoholism and eventually severe mental illness. She was committed to an institution where she lived until her death.

The Attorney General my aunt married was Thomas E. Knight, Jr., Greensboro native and infamous prosecutor of the Scottsboro Boys who were charged with raping a white woman in the 1930s. His relentless prosecution, despite a judge originally dismissing the charges and obvious flaws resulting in repeated retrials, reinforced stereotypical views of white

Alabamians as racists. Knight died before the final trials found three of the original nine guilty. Many felt they were innocent. In 2013, the Alabama Board of Pardons granted them full posthumous pardons. Alabama's Legislature had to pass a new law allowing the Board to review the case, and the decision was hailed as a testimony to change.

I believe my aunts and my father were deeply affected by being in the shadows of their ancestors or by over-reaching family pride in the lineage. The message portrayed in Jack's whispered words to me had staying power in their lives. My father's only brother was an eccentric crusty uncle, but an affable character, solid family man, good provider, and not possessed by alcohol—an exception in his family. With due respect for proponents of weighty genetics, my own experience and common sense tells me that the reasons one person turns ill and another goes straight ahead in life relate to both genetic and environmental factors, and proportionate effects vary with individuals. There are also the important factors of self-determination and, for those of faith, divine intervention. At any rate, there were times when some members of my family relied on ancestral glories or imagined riches—*being better than them*—and may have had little else. Not everyone has a storied and proud ancestral history, but everyone strives for something—real or imagined, good or bad—on which to base self-esteem.

Before and for a while after Jack's death, her home was staffed by black women, so-called servants. Unlike Sarah, my mother's helper, they were required to wear white uniforms and caps and to maintain formal behavior, especially when visitors were present. To me, they seemed the last vestiges of slavery. Regardless of appearances and even an inheritance from her endowed side of the family, Jack lived a considerably reduced lifestyle compared to previous generations. Her fortunes continued to diminish until my proud grandmother was forced to take in boarders.

Various business endeavors of my humble and hard-working uncle-by-marriage Scott may have helped Jack's household income, but times were not easy. Uncle Scott took over the service station after accidentally blowing off his arm with a shotgun. In perhaps the most traumatic event I experienced as a child, my mother and I found him screaming in the front yard, his arm gushing blood, and rushed him to the hospital. For years thereafter, he endured pain but worked hard without complaint, forced to work using a mechanical arm not nearly so advanced as they are today.

When I was a child, my father was somewhat functional as an alcoholic. He was a valued employee who immersed himself in work, but he was not a very functional father. He worked nights and slept during much of the daytime, rarely involved in my activities. Like his sisters, he was not overtly destructive so much as passively so, at least by the time I came along. His erratic behavior was rough, but I was spared the worst. However, by the time he was sober at age fifty-nine, I was an energetic twelve-year-old, and he did not have what it took to engage with me. After years of his alcohol abuse and tragedies befalling two older sons, he was burned out. He was not proactive with me, and could not express his emotions directly; the best I ever saw was a resisted tear on rare occasions. My father loved me in his way, but I never felt loved by him growing up, something so important for children and lacking by too many in our society today.

As the youngest by ten years of four siblings, I was quite unanticipated. It pleased my dear mother to smile gently and say I was not the caboose but the trailer. As for self-esteem or security issues, on top of my father's struggles with alcohol and being a father—plus the challenges of my diabetic condition—I had a few more downers. Losing his grip on reality while in the Korean conflict, my oldest brother was institutionalized most of his adult life with paranoid schizophrenia. The next oldest brother served time in prison for committing a federal crime in a position of trust in our little community. Both brothers were popular, respected men with a lot of promise before their difficulties. My sister, by age much closer to our brothers and their crises as well as my father's struggles, suffered more from the family wounds. She overcame through her faith and a good marriage to a good man. As for me, sometimes trailers avoid the worst by simply trailing.

Everyone has downers in life. My academic training gave me facts about that, but counseling many people over years helped me really see that so many others have much more luggage than I ever carried. My experience helping others also helped me see how so many people suffer from self-esteem issues. I came to believe that being compelled or striving to consider ourselves better than others sets us up for a fall, whatever exact shape that may take. Genuine self-esteem must be inward, I think. Years after his prison time, my brother asked me, "Haven't you always felt there's supposed to be something better for you?" It is a long way down to the realities of life from inflated expectations. Throughout my time living at home, there were no substantive family or community conversations about either brother's misfortunes in life—always talked around but not about. A lot of families do lip service or less in addressing real pain that surrounds them and even sometimes engulfs them. I believe my family's ancestral treasures and an emphasis on being *better than them* was a poor gap filler and worse. Instead of boosting self-esteem in the face of life's negatives, the downers, it actually added fuel to the fire of self-degradation in the long run.

Another thing I learned from my counseling was how alcohol becomes progressively more important to people for various reasons and insidiously grows into a full-fledged addiction, a disease. It can even be a cultural disease in families to the point that members not captured by it can feel that they are on the outside looking in. While I do not see drinking in and of itself as a negative, I have seen so many individuals and families broken and even destroyed by dependence on it. I have also seen many in denial about it, and my family was one of those.

Somehow, regardless of the cultural and personal luggage and rage I carried that day of the march in 1965, I made the right decision to not strike out. While a momentary bad decision can begin a downward life spiral, the right decision at that same moment can be a positive turning point for life. Who knows when his or her effect on a child may make the difference at a crucial time like that? Many have been seemingly set up for a fall by weak gap-fillers, but releasing the grip—or determining what's at your core, what you value most—is still an individual decision. Jesus's statement from the NIV version of the Bible-sixth chapter of Matthew, verse 21, is on point: *For where your treasure is, there your heart will be also.*

My mother, Mary, believed in prayer. A former schoolteacher, she was always the reader, the poetic storyteller, the singer of wake-up songs that were medicine to my young soul, songs like "The Sun Shines Bright on Little Red Wing." She persisted with that stuff, amazing when I think about my teen years in particular! My mother came from humble beginnings in

Pickens County where her mother was left alone with five children after her first husband died and the second had heavy problems resulting in a divorce. In contrast to Jack, this grandmother gave piano lessons and took in sewing jobs to support the children. As a Christian, she laid no claim to personal glory, present or past.

I'm sure it's no surprise to learn that my flip-side grandmother Jack had difficulty accepting my mother as my father's chosen mate. You can also believe that she was resisting one of the potential anecdotes for the internal struggles of many in our family—much-needed humility! Fact is, by including my mother, my hard-working uncle by marriage who lived with my grandmother, and a few others who also came in by marriage, our proud family took healthy doses of the antidote that paid dividends much later.

Standing on that curb in 1965, I gripped a weapon and considered violent action in the heat of the moment. Loaded with my own issues of self-esteem, I also carried the anger and resentments of generations and a culture. I was one individual enslaved by many influences around me, seemingly far beyond my control. My treasure was fool's gold. Yet, there was my mother, and the spark of decency was also nurtured by other influences in my life growing up in Greensboro—the weight of some only appreciated by me years after that day.

12

THE DOCTOR, THE CAD,
AND ANGELIC TEACHERS

Not every white person in my hometown was likely to take up a rubber hose or a tire iron as some of us did that summer day of the march. Among those of us who did, many were not total reprobates, and the worst were not necessarily irredeemable. Not everything in my hometown was about racism, either. Good people had a good influence on me. Trauma in our family and the lack of a good connection with my father made that influence extremely important. I believe it also paid off eventually as I adjusted my perspective about others. Unlike my unmistakable understanding of Coach Key's position, I had virtually no knowledge of the racial attitudes of most of these people. Considering our culture then, I believe that the silence itself—in combination with exemplary lives and acts of kindness—spoke of some exceptionality, and was positively influential for me in terms of how I eventually came to view myself related to others.

Two physicians practiced in Greensboro during my growing-up years, Dr. Anderson and Dr. McAdory, who took over much of Anderson's practice when he retired. Dr. McAdory diagnosed my diabetes and sent me to the University of Alabama in Birmingham Hospital. It was not just that he did that and not just that he later took enough interest in my potential to help me get a vocational rehabilitation scholarship: In fact, I don't think Dr. McAdory ever really knew how much he did for me in a simple way. Unlike Coach Key, Dr. McAdory was always verbally subtle, even quiet. However, he had a way of saying just the right thing at the right moment, and his quiet manner was accompanied by a ready smile and a pat on the back when needed.

Dr. McAdory was, in effect, our team doctor. He attended many football practices. Once, when I was at home sick, Dr. McAdory came to visit, and told me Coach Key had made the statement at practice that, "If Otts was here, he would show you how to do it!" It may seem such a small thing, but I credit Dr. McAdory for telling me something a fifteen-year-old struggling diabetic with a difficult family situation and self-esteem issues needed to hear. I honestly believe he felt I needed it. He was right, and I replayed his words many times over the years as needed. It was the amazing power of a few encouraging words at the right time. I went back to school and practiced the next day—not giving up before giving it my best. It was important because I needed to face my fading dream without regret, and Dr. McAdory helped me do it. Football meant a lot to many of us, but especially to those of us without consistent father figures. We were influenced by people like the good doctor and good coaches like Key whose concerns for us went beyond the field of competition. The same is true for many kids today.

What does the incident with Dr. McAdory or the quoted words of Coach Key have to do with racial discrimination and the change in my perspective? It relates to self-worth or self-esteem, something we all need and some may even strive for over many years, consciously or not. I am not suggesting that resolving a self-worth issue resolves the issue of racism—just that it is an important factor for many people in terms of how they see themselves relative to others. The degree to which our quest for self-worth is truly resolved may affect our compulsion to elevate self relative to others (call it a fake self-esteem) and related racial perspectives at some point for some people. Substantive, healthy self-esteem promotes a view of others that does not have to diminish them in order to elevate self, actually a form of dependence.

Looking back, I now understand that even bad examples helped me in that they provided a contrast or a truth once I opened up to potentials outside the bubble. Once, when I was in my teens, a fellow in Greensboro exposed some of my friends and me to his view on the issue of race. He was from *up north*. It never mattered what state they came from, people coming from anywhere above the Mason-Dixon line were from *up north*. This white man was probably in his mid-thirties. I don't know why he came to the South, but he quickly gained a reputation for being a carouser of the worst type—by all accounts, a womanizer and inclined to be violent when confronted. He was definitely not inclined to cover up his indiscretions, a big exception in my hometown!

One day, a few of my friends and I happened upon this guy at a time and place when he and we had nothing to do, so we talked. Of course, we often had nothing better to do than be intrigued with anything different, and he sure fit that bill. He seemed to be in a good mood, and told us various stories about things in which we had no interest. We were more interested in his experience with another subject, but waited for it to surface for fear of going there. Finally, one of the guys broke down and awkwardly said something about sex. This Northerner jumped on it like a fly on sugar, proceeding to give lurid details about his sexual exploits. Even when one of us was lying to the others, none of us had ever heard anything like this. Then, he came to the astounding topic of having sexual intercourse with women who were black! We were absolutely floored by one statement that I cannot recall word for word, but it went something like this: "A lot of white guys say they would never have sex with a black woman. Well, I say they're all the same inside." We were absolutely dumbfounded that even somebody from *up north* dared to consider black women equal to white women, anatomically correct or not! Of course, as brave as we thought we were, we did not dare confront him with our disgust.

Now, it was not that this cad taught me something profound at face value. However, it was another piece of my memory that would not go away. I would later rerun it in the series of race-related incidents that took place as I was growing up. It was only pertinent as I chose it to be and as a contrast to the general context of my life at the time. As I matured, I determined which pieces meant what to me. We all have those choices, and such experiences are what we choose them to be for our detriment or benefit. Later, I realized that what the cad said applied in a different way than intended: As it is easy to identify with the love Mammy felt for the little girl she had raised, it is easy to understand that we are all the same on the inside, in our hearts, regardless of externals like skin color. Coming to change my views on race and maturing them was much like piecing together a puzzle. People and institutions contributed pieces, and faith had a lot to do with maturing my understanding into daily life. I hope that man from up north changed. I know it's possible.

Definitely on the flip side from the cad, I was truly blessed when it came to having sensitive and very capable English and literature instructors in junior high and high school. My mother's love for reading and her enduring gentleness and patience was greatly complemented by these teachers' approach to life and learning. In junior high, I was regaled by the very concerned and enthusiastic Miss Evelyn Anderson, daughter of the same Dr. Anderson who delivered me into the world. Evelyn Anderson was a woman who lost the use of her legs to an errant gunshot as a child. Miss Anderson taught from a constantly reclined, elbow-supported position on a motor-less four-wheel bed or gurney that she adroitly wheeled around her classroom and through the hallways of Greensboro High, requiring occasional assistance. In the days of my adolescence, I was largely inappreciative for her enthusiasm, contagiously consistent smile, and obvious concern for every student.

Miss Anderson did not have legs that worked, but she lived life in a wonderful way. I did not get it at the time, but her attitude about life later came home to me as sheer inspiration—a magnificent piece of the puzzle. When I picture her today, I do not see that gurney. I see a genuine, big smile. Evelyn Anderson was posthumously inducted into the Alabama Women's Hall of Fame, and the following quote from the organization's website says a lot:

> She began teaching in 1948 as an "unofficial art teacher in a vacant classroom" at Greensboro High school because an Alabama law prohibited hiring seriously handicapped teachers. Miss Anderson inspired a State Senator and the Alabama State School Superintendent to work for the passage of a new law (enacted in 1953) to repeal the prohibition. She then became the first seriously handicapped professional hired by the Alabama public schools (1954). . . . Pioneering the rights of those with physical handicaps, she inspired the city of Greensboro to provide accommodations for the mobility disabled before being required by law to do so. She won numerous awards and honors, including Outstanding Educator (1974), Outstanding Counselor of the Year (1975-76) and the Alabama Handicapped Professional Woman of the Year (1977). She served

on Alabama Governor's Committee on Employment of the Handicapped (1977). In 1976, Alabama Educational (now Public) Television aired a short documentary film about her life as an educator and inspiration for children. . . .

Miss Mary Martin was a students' teacher. Older than Miss Anderson, she was perhaps in her fifties when I was a Greensboro High Senior, but nobody could possibly think of her as fifty. Her positive, generous spirit and free smile were contagious. Her love for the subject she taught spread all over the place. Literature formed Miss Martin's backdrop for life, and she cared about students no matter who they were. She loved to challenge students during extra-curricula activities, including introducing us to the fine art of Scrabble playing. It was her way of helping us have fun and learn at the same time. How could anyone interest students in such things when they had other options? You had to know her.

Miss Martin gave me a keen interest in literature that has faded somewhat over the years. (Shame on you, she would say with a broad, understanding smile.) In class, she read literature with joy—often playing a part appropriate to the book or poem we were studying. Miss Martin could easily have been an actress. This was one lively teacher who just did her thing naturally. She transmitted something of lifetime importance and introduced me to the likes of Keats, Burns, and Tennyson. While my mother could be credited with helping me gain an early interest in reading, sports and girls had supplanted that by the last two years of high school. Before Miss Martin's class, I read literature mostly out of compulsion; what I read voluntarily with enthusiasm included such substantive works as *The Baseball Almanac*!

Mary Martin enticed me to begin reading Tennyson's poetry on my own time, unassigned! My friends, fellow students, and family did not know this. It was contrary to the image I was trying to project at the time. One thing led to another, and my senior year was very progressive academically. College looked realistic because I met Mr. Tennyson through Miss Martin. There is more to it than that, though, something spiritual. While our Presbyterian minister waxed eloquent and long, and though I went to many a Sunday School class (hearing Brer Rabbit stories mostly), by the time I was a junior in high school, I didn't attend church much anymore. I did not know until much later that stories such as those told by the Sunday School teacher were part of a rich oral tradition of storytelling that was brought from Africa by slaves and adapted to fit life in America.

My dad's own lackadaisical attitude toward religion made my absence from church a lot easier. Even though I was approaching a time when I would claim to be an atheist, I was helped to move toward spirituality by Mary Martin. I began to think on a different level, and introspection became meaningful. I had no idea where the journey was taking me, but imagination even gained purpose beyond escape. The words of Tennyson touched my heart, and helped me get more in touch with my mortality later. . . . *and let there be no moaning of the bar when I put out to sea.* Until being touched by these spiritual tones, I had shut off my mind to such considerations because they called me out of the box of my security. I was beginning to reckon with the questions of life that we so often prefer to avoid. I even began to write poetry and essays that were more therapeutic than anything, secretive writings of course. I am truly thankful today for a wonderful teacher who helped me think out of my box—and out of the bubble to some degree—to glimpse the shadow of God.

Could Miss Martin, Dr. McAdory, or Miss Anderson have known they helped me change my perspective about where I stood relative to other people—to see beyond skin color and begin to value the minds and souls of others? I doubt it. Over the course of lifetimes, people usually never know what their words and examples truly mean to those they influence. In my experience, racial matters were never directly addressed by these good people, even when those matters were on the front burner of life in our town. If any of them saw things differently from the cultural norm and expressed their views, they would probably not have remained in positions of influence for long, at least not in my hometown. My conviction is that they helped me break the surly bonds of racism.

13

SARAH, HAMMERING HANK, SEEDS, AND MOCKINGBIRDS

The march to the courthouse I witnessed and the one preempted when demonstrators were bused to Selma both started at St. Matthew AME Church on the short block of Morse Street and then onto Main Street. At the opposite end of Morse and just past the church, a few houses were visible across North Street where Morse intersected it. As opposed to more substantial houses in town, these were unpainted wooden structures with tin roofs and probably no more than four or five rooms maximum per house. Sarah lived in one of those. The house is no longer there, but well-remembered from the times my mother and I waited in the car for her to ride with us to work at our home. She was generally sitting in a rocking chair out on that little wooden front porch—a short, rotund woman with very dark skin and a broad smile. Sarah was my mother's helper at the house on weekdays and more at times. Completely dedicated to our family, she had a positive outlook on life, not unlike my mother.

As the youngest of four children, with the nearest in age ten years older than me, I was practically an only child from age eight. I spent a lot of time with Sarah. She was not my nanny, but could have been. She washed clothes, cleaned the house, helped my mother cook, and did numerous other things including watching me when mom occasionally had somewhere to go without me. Sarah always did what my mother said, but they functioned as a team most of the time.

Unlike my mother who had a ready smile but did not laugh a lot, Sarah found it easy to laugh. One of the most endearing things about her for me was the fact that she found it so easy to laugh at the home comedian. That would be me, and she laughed even when I was not very funny. She loved to sing or hum gospel music while working. Sarah was also talkative, but there was never talk of politics or government or anything at all outside of Greensboro for that matter, except talk of God. To her, God was good, and she was blessed. Sarah heard a lot of racial slurs in my home, never—to my knowledge—from my mother but certainly from my father and me. I don't remember any of it being directed at her, and she never reacted visibly. Surely she gritted her teeth at some of the things we said. Of course, I had no insights into her personal life and relationships where such things were likely aired—as presented in the popular book and movie of same title, *The Help*.

I was a rough-and-tumble boy, inclined to mischief and subject to stitches. Sarah supplemented my mother's efforts in dealing with youthful pains, physical and otherwise. She was there when I went through the family traumas, things my mother tried to shield me from instead of helping me face them. My father never knew what to do, and my family did not talk feelings much. Sarah never took the lead, but she seemed to sing the most soothing gospel songs when I was in pain, offering occasional brief words of assurance. Often, she would just be there, but she legitimately cared. It mattered.

People like Sarah can make such a difference by being at the right place at the right time. The payoff in my life was not so visible then, but it was part of the puzzle later. It's so difficult now to think that, as a boy, I might not have known Sarah's last name. I sought to know it after years of obliviousness. It's never too late, even after a person's death, to call an honorable name. Her name was Sarah Roberson, and she lived in Sawyerville in later years. She was a good person.

There were also some who affected my attitudes from a distance. I remember being very young when we first got a black and white TV. It quickly became a focal point at home. For me, TV sports was a great haven. Looking back at my most impressionable years, I consider the examples and impressions left by such icons as Sheriff Andy Griffith of Mayberry, and they pale against that of one particular sports star. I doubt he ever set foot in my hometown, and I've not met him to this day. Yet he made a difference. Some years ago, I wrote a piece about Hank Aaron that was published below his picture in my city newspaper, the *Mobile Press Register*. Mobile was Hank's hometown. I want to share the article here because I believe it clearly states my point about Hammering Hank's influence.

A recent note in Sound Off questioned the contributions of Hank Aaron to Mobile. I want to offer a retort based on a subject with which I am somewhat familiar: me. As a white boy growing up in a small Alabama town, I was surrounded by influences that promoted racism. This is not to say that my hometown was all bad. It was a good place to grow up, but it was flawed—just like people. For me, there was one notable outside influence, and that was professional baseball. I loved the game, the baseball cards, and the speculation about the best players.

It may seem strange today that my favorite team was the Milwaukee Braves, but the fact that they were the National League's Yankee killers provides the most logical explanation, those two legendary teams facing off in consecutive World Series. My favorite player was a gritty third baseman, Eddie Mathews, recently deceased. At least, I told the guys he was my favorite. There was one reason Mathews held this position: The other Milwaukee Brave who captured my attention as a twelve-year old was a black man. His name was Hank Aaron, and he was indeed the Hammer when it came to hitting a baseball. He was also a speed merchant on the base paths and an excellent fielder. He did all those things in a masterful way, but there was something else that drew this little boy's attention to Hank Aaron, and I want to share it with you.

In Hank Aaron, I saw a man of quiet, humble character who worked very hard to be the best at his profession. You see, to me, Hank Aaron's strength has always been his humility, and his pride has been apparent in the way he carries himself and has endured under pressure. I lived in a place where a white boy identifying with a black man was grounds for sheer lunacy, but I was not crazy. I liked Hank Aaron. It had nothing to do with color, and everything to do with class. Later, when he was striving for Babe Ruth's record, I knew little about the threats on his life and family. I didn't hear the racial slurs. I saw a man still quietly striving to give his best, regardless.

Hank Aaron was my favorite player, belatedly claimed, whose example put my feet on a bridge leading toward seeing my fellow man in a different way. Oh sure, a lot more water passed under that bridge in my life. However, for one twelve-year old, Hank came along at a time when I needed a favorite who just happened to be black. In my heart, I knew he was my favorite all along. Today, I can say it with pride. That's a difference. That's a contribution to our community.

In my view, the return on investments that a real champion makes in the lives of others, especially children, is very meaningful. Hank Aaron never gave anything to our community? I'll let others tell you about money and material assets. I can tell you that Hank Aaron's investment in my life has been significant, and I like to think that it continues to pay dividends in the lives of those in our community whom I may influence. Thank you, Hank.

Hank Aaron and Sarah Robinson, each in their unique way, helped me overcome racism as pieces of the puzzle came clear down the road.

The verbal assaults on Principal Key and Martin Luther King helped me in ways the barbershop crowd would never know. Over subsequent years, I now realize I was beginning to associate these two men in my mind. Meanwhile, the connecting line between my grandmother's whispered words and me was beginning to blur. It was not the end of my old views, but different seeds for thought were planted. If a person is not being bombarded daily with reinforcements, even a single seed of thought may have opportunity to grow—again, over time.

You never can tell which seeds you sow will grow and bear fruit. I guess the essence of it is that we are all teachers to somebody, and the greatest lessons—positive and negative—are indeed caught and not taught. I really don't think the seeding had anything to do with class content in college. I did spend more time talking to people with varying views, and the give-and-take exposed me to different thinking than I had encountered before on a number of subjects. It seems we were all philosophers in those days. However, very little regarded race relations at that point, mostly just a matter of seeing other possibilities worth considering beyond the bubble. That's a scary thought for many parents releasing their children to college, but individuals need to grow as individuals.

Aside from the barbershop haranguing, subtle changes in my perspective found an unexpected sounding board at home that first summer back from college. One night, we were watching *The Ed Sullivan Show*, and Sammy Davis Jr. was the guest star. My father cursed to the rooftop and literally jumped out of his chair to change the channel. It grated on his nerves to see a black man performing on TV. Athletes did not generate the same reaction, but he was not a big baseball and football fan like his son. I actually spoke up to say something like, "Why don't you quit that? It's not doing any good!" He didn't take kindly to my commentary.

It may not seem more than just a father-son spat, but something was going on inside me that I did not fully understand. In addition to the usual attempt to establish my independence, I saw that my father's reaction was not proportionate to reality. I remember enjoying the versatility of Davis, and the fact that he was black was not very important to my enjoyment. That summer I was not yet ready to see accomplished black people as worthy of equality, but I was ready to enjoy their skills. One of the reasons I made fewer visits home after that summer was the widening gap between my father and me. The shame of such avoidance is that others suffer, and it is generally good for all involved to express differences to each other in a family. In regard to boys and such relationships with their fathers, I was not alone. As many have lamented, I only wish I had been able to share these feelings with my dad while he was still alive.

College football was also a source of the seeds of doubt and change for me. Football is almost on par with religion in my home state, and I'm not sure why it became so important to so many Alabamians. Maybe we just needed to be good at something relative to the rest of the nation. Maybe we needed something diverse people could rally around. Regardless of how it happened, football became a sport that preoccupied and continues to preoccupy many of us. Most Alabamians are fans of either the University of Alabama or Auburn University, a lot of us shamelessly passionate. Perhaps the most significant seeds of change planted by football relates to racism.

Back in the days when I admired Green Bay Packers quarterback Bart Starr because he had played for Alabama, there were no black players at either of our revered state institutions. While important that black students were able to attend previously all-white institutions, it was also important that black football players began to earn athletic scholarships and represent all the tradition and accomplishment of storied football programs. The University of Alabama was an institution where fans practically drooled at the prospect of winning Rose Bowl games in the early days when the Crimson Tide dominated teams from other areas of the country. In football, through the Tide's all-white teams, the South had indeed risen again.

Today, legendary Coach Paul *Bear* Bryant's shadow is still evident all over the UA campus and among fans and alumni all over Alabama despite his death in 1983. All you have to do is look for the abundance of houndstooth-patterned items, emulating Bryant's famous hat pattern. He was already a very successful and revered coach by the time he began to recruit the best athletes from predominantly black high schools. When Coach Bryant recruited and signed running back Wilbur Jackson in 1970, I was in my first and only year of law school. By that time, I was on the verge of forming a new perspective on race but was still not quite there. A father figure to many football players and others, Bryant's TV show and down-home, self-effacing approach endeared him to students, faculty, alumni, and fans.

The Bear's persona and influence spread through all the communities where he recruited players and came to know community and state leaders. It was said that if he ran for governor he would be elected by a landslide. I'm not sure what that says about our state, but I believe it. In fact, I am not at all sure anyone but the Bear could have integrated Alabama football effectively and without a lot of noise.

When it comes to true social change, all the programs, lawsuits, even Supreme Court rulings pale in comparison to solid unassailable examples set by leaders and everyday people. Coach Paul Bear Bryant was another imperfect hero, but he was still heroic to people who needed or wanted a hero. He did not preach on the evils of racism or pass laws. All he did was field the best team he could, regardless of skin color, and demonstrate the same color blindness about his assistant coaches, players, and their families. I was impressed with the football, and saw the character of many players who happened to be black, not just good football players, but good people.

Most people are familiar with the book and subsequent movie *To Kill a Mockingbird*, which came out in 1960 and 1962, respectively. The book was written by Monroeville, Alabama, native Harper Lee. The one-two punch of book and movie at the right time influenced many people to become part of the movement to end racism. Star Gregory Peck and movie crew came to Monroeville to scope out the scene and meet author Harper Lee who based elements of the book on her hometown. As moving and penetrating as I regard both book and film now, I doubt that either converted many segregationists like me in 1965. Apart from some religious awakening or conversion, most of us were probably changed in increments through the examples of others and seeds planted in various ways. We grew in cultural self-awareness and into the capacity to be open to other views. People, events, literature, TV, movies, and other influences gave us pause for thought and helped us slowly emerge from our bubbles.

The book and movie did not play into my thinking. I don't know for sure but believe the movie *To Kill a Mockingbird* was not even shown in Greensboro when I was a teenager. That could be expected. At least, I didn't see it until years later. My wife and I have visited Monroeville twice to take in the play based on the book, a crucial part of which is performed in the old courthouse. It is a memorable experience, and credit goes to local actors and crew (all who hold regular jobs). The town has embraced this as an important part of its heritage, and an international traveling version of the play has received acclaim. The first time we attended, it was my pleasure to serve as a member of the jury composed of men from the audience—quite an experience! I hope parents will help their children, as they mature, to have the opportunity to dwell on a book as rich as *To Kill a Mockingbird* or to see the movie at the least. I also hope many will take in the play in Monroeville and see the related exhibits in the old courthouse.

If I had read the book or seen the movie when young, it may not have changed my thinking, but it could well have been a significant seed. Whether town characters or someone who was different only by skin color, meta-phorical mockingbirds lived in my hometown, doing no harm and actually doing good. As Atticus Finch said, . . . *it's a sin to kill a mockingbird.* I take that to mean it's morally wrong to consign good and innocent people like white Boo Radley or black Tom Robinson to oblivion or to some form of inhumanity just because they are different—as I did in 1965.

14

LEAVE THE GRAND DRAGON ALONE!

In 1965, the Ku Klux Klan did not hold many public meetings like the one in Greensboro that summer. Anonymously hooded and cloaked in darkness, they generally used secrecy and related mystique to their advantage. During the day, they held regular jobs and, in daylight, you didn't know when a KKK member might be watching you. The KKK idea was to reinforce racism and discourage public expression of contrary views. Civil rights activities drew the Klan out in the sixties, but they were more visible in the fifties, always cloaked of course.

One Saturday, when I was maybe eight or nine, my mother was driving us downtown when she stopped in the middle of Main Street. A few white-robed, hooded men were blocking the road, holding buckets and collecting cash. One approached my mother's open window to ask her for a contribution. I don't recall her reply, but I know that she did not put anything in the bucket. If she rejected the cause, I didn't know it. She told me the man was a member of the Ku Klux Klan, and I don't think I asked my mother any more questions about them. The one negative that stuck with me was the scary getup.

I do not recall ever seeing another hooded Klansman in person, but I heard a lot about their exploits. I enjoyed KKK stories—viewing them as taking up the fallen cause of the Confederacy to preserve the South. By the time I was in high school, I had developed some skepticism due to the secrecy that surrounded them—a sort of come-on-out-and-fight thing on my part. At the same time, talk was that the feds would shut them down if identities were known. The underdog argument was effective in quelling skepticism because we saw ourselves as victims of the same perpetrators.

The Ku Klux Klan has been around since shortly after the Civil War ended.

Early leaders fought for the Confederacy, and their primary objective was to contest anything that might give black people more influence, voting power being a prime example. Much Klan momentum resulted from post-Civil War Reconstruction military rule and intrusion by Northern carpetbaggers who sought to profit from the South's dire circumstances and the cooperative Southerners, called scalawags, who worked with them. Due to the war and the aftermath of Reconstruction, the South went from the most promising area of the U.S. economically to the most impoverished, and white resentments boiled. Investigations authorized by Congress demonstrated that the typical KKK approach involved threats of violence and violence itself.

After Reconstruction ended and reinforcements for white control were established politically (including prohibitions in Alabama's new state constitution of 1901 that essentially blocked many blacks from voting), the KKK lost its rallying point. That is, until World War I provided a new one and the Klan rose again, this time capitalizing on hatred toward Jews, Catholics, Socialists, and Communists. Hatred fuels hatred, and within a year, a silent movie, D. W. Griffith's *Birth of a Nation,* which portrayed black people during the Reconstruction era as violent and untrustworthy (exceptions being those who were still submissive to whites), reinforced fears of black people and bolstered the KKK itself: it was even used in KKK recruitment and training!

I had not seen *Birth of a Nation* until a few years ago when I was astounded by the utter audacity of the film. The production portrayed the KKK as heroic rescuers, defenders of the honorable and victimized whites, and even referenced the Southern white population's *Aryan birthright*—a reference that was edited out in some later versions. The inflammatory film was based on two popular books and a play, and the title of one of the books took me back to a sermon from the past: *The Leopard's Spots, a Romance of the White Man's Burden.*

Its popularity fueled by the movie and by fears generated by World War I, the Klan's national membership reached over four million by 1925 with well over a hundred thousand in Alabama. Cloaked Klansmen were rarely publicly identified or charged with crimes. Even when linked with violence, they were not likely to be charged with crimes or convicted by juries if they were charged, thanks to sympathetic local law enforcement, judges, and juries. In 1944, as the fervor of hatred diminished and some high-profile Klansmen were finally convicted, the organization formally disbanded, but once again, it was only hibernating. The emerging civil rights movement of the late 1950s and early 1960s awakened the beast, and the Klan was revived for its third life to oppose the calls for voting rights for blacks and other civil and human rights reforms.

A 1954 speech by Dr. E. P. Pruitt, then Grand Dragon of the Federated Klans of Alabama, was revealing—the excerpt below (quoted in an article, Ku Klux Klan, by John Simkin, Spartacus Educational website) is now so disgusting to me that it makes me feel ill.

> The Klan don't hate nobody! In fact, the Klan is the good nigger's best friend. If the nigger will devote his energies to becoming a better, more useful nigger, rather than the dupe of Northern interests who have caused him to misconstrue his social standing, he will reap the rewards of industry, instead of the disappointments of ambition unobtainable!
>
> Southern whites, occupying that super-position assigned them by the Creator, are justifiably hostile to any race that attempts to drag them down to its own level! Therefore let the nigger be wise in leaving the ballot in the hands of a dominant sympathetic race, since he is far better off as a political eunuch in the house of his friends, than a voter rampant in the halls of his enemies! . . .

As an adolescent, I harbored thoughts that my father may have been involved in the KKK. Finally, I questioned him directly. He dodged the question, only reinforcing my suspicions. As a Mason for some years, he attended secretive meetings never discussed in our home. Many have asserted that sometimes Masonic (or Freemasonry) activities in the South were a Klan front—that leaders of the original KKK in Pulaski, Tennessee were Masons, as well as a number of subsequent leaders; there were also local rumors about the Masons being a front for the Klan.

I never learned anything from my father or any other Mason about what they did. He kept Masonic items in a box that I pilfered more than once.

It contained an apron-like silk white cloth with the blue Masonic symbol, a ring with the symbol, and some other items. Later, when I learned that a gun was one prerequisite for KKK membership, I wondered about a secluded derringer my father never referenced. He found me exploring contents of the box once and was very angry. Nothing directly connected my father's Masonic activities with the KKK, but there were rumors, and during the years of heightened KKK activity, he attended some long Masonic meetings at night. As for Freemasonry today, their leaders repudiate any claims that the two organizations were ever connected. Regardless of formalities, it seems entirely possible to me that some local Masonic chapters could have been connected with the KKK in the past. Secrecy may limit absolute conclusions, but it also feeds doubts.

The history of the civil rights movement in Alabama was characterized by justice delayed, particularly regarding the KKK, which only delayed healing and held back the progress of racial harmony. On Sunday, September 15, 1963, a white man was seen placing a box under the steps of the Sixteenth Street Baptist Church in Birmingham. The bomb exploded, and four young black girls, eleven-year-old Denise McNair, and fourteen-year-olds Addie Mae Collins, Carole Robertson, and Cynthia Wesley were killed during Sunday school. A KKK member named Robert Chambliss was charged, but found not guilty of murder; he received a hundred-dollar fine and a six-month jail sentence for unlawful possession of dynamite. Years later, Alabama Attorney General Bill Baxley reviewed evidentiary materials in FBI case files, and in 1977, Chambliss was retried, found guilty, and finally sentenced to life in prison where he died in 1985.

Still, justice lagged even more. In 2001, thirty-eight years after the Sixteen Street Baptist Church was bombed, the FBI said it was the responsibility of a Ku Klux Klan splinter group that included Chambliss and three other white men. Herman Frank Cash had already died. The other two, Thomas Blanton Jr. and Bobby Frank Cherry, were convicted of the murders of those innocent girls. Both were sentenced to finish their lives in prison after being found guilty in 2001 and 2002—almost forty years after the bombing!

In 1981, the trial of a black man charged with the murder of a white policeman took place in Mobile. The jury did not reach a verdict. Members of the local KKK believed the reason was that some members of the jury were black. As recorded on the website of the *African American Registry*, Bennie Hays, the second-highest ranking official in the Klan in Alabama at the time, said "If a black man can get away with killing a white man, we ought to be able to get away with killing a black man."

Henry Hays (Bennie's son) and a friend went out looking for a way to exact revenge. Cruising around Mobile, they spotted nineteen-year-old Michael Donald walking home. They forced him into the car, took him to another county, mercilessly beat him, and slit his throat. For show, they hung his body on a tree back in Mobile. A police investigation determined that the killing resulted from a drug deal gone sour, but Donald's mother knew he was not into drugs, and she was determined to prove them wrong.

Thomas Figures, then Assistant United States Attorney in Mobile, got the FBI to check out the case. Henry Hay's friend confessed to violating Donald's civil rights, and turned state's evidence on Hays who was tried, convicted of murder, and sentenced to death. After a series of appeals, Hays was finally executed in June of 1997—justice delayed for eighteen years.

Following are some meaningful comments written by Frances Coleman in her opinion piece for the *Mobile Register* on July 1, 1997, five days before Hays was to be executed:

> The execution will rip the scab from the old, deep, nasty wound of racism, which in the 20th-century South alternately heals and festers. It will fester again this week as residents of the Heart of Dixie re-live the brutal death of 19-year-old Michael Donald. . . .
>
> Most vivid, though, is the contrast between fiction and reality. Michael Donald was murdered—beaten to death with a tree limb—not in the 1930s or '40s, even in the 1960s, but in 1981. Such things weren't supposed to happen almost 30 years after the Supreme Court declared "separate but equal" unconstitutional, and nearly 20 years after the Civil Rights Act of 1964.
>
> Nor were they supposed to happen in Mobile, which in the 1960s had somehow managed to avoid the racial violence that erupted in Selma and Birmingham.

Black men kidnapped and beaten, their bodies strung up in a tree? That was something that happened on the dark back roads of Dallas County or over in the Mississippi Delta, not in Alabama's second-largest city.

But hate crimes aren't constrained by time, place or suppositions. . . .

Death penalty advocates tout execution as a deterrent to crime, and maybe it is in some respects. Henry Hays' death, though, will serve mostly as a sad commentary on a society that in 1997—less than three years from the turn of the century—is having to electrocute a man for murdering another man, solely because of the color of his skin.

In 1987, ten years before Hays was executed, the Southern Poverty Law Center filed a civil suit against the Ku Klux Klan in Alabama on behalf of Michael Donald's mother, Beulah Mae Donald. The KKK was held responsible for the lynching of Mrs. Donald's son, and ordered to pay seven million dollars. This forced them to surrender all assets, including national headquarters in Tuscaloosa. It was justice, but delayed once again while old wounds festered and even became generational.

Hamner Cobbs, the outspoken editor of the *Greensboro Watchman*, obviously thought very little of Reverend King or President Kennedy, but to his credit, he was also no fan of the KKK and Grand Dragon Robert Shelton. Shelton was the one stirring white passions in his Greensboro speech in 1965. Cobbs, in an October 21, 1965, editorial titled "Leave Him Alone," first directed his attention to the KKK and Shelton and then to Congress by saying this:

> Our attitudes toward the Klan and its overall purpose of saving the South have not altered. We still regard it as a cheap organization with a few zealous but misled people. . . . On the other hand, the current drive against Shelton and his crowd, both by Congress and the Johnson administration, is silly and unworthy. Congress is now threatening to cite Shelton for contempt because he will not turn over to that body certain of his papers. The national administration, all the way from Katzenbach to that Alabama stooge, Richmond Flowers, is threatening Shelton and the Klan.
>
> Shelton isn't worth it. He is just another cheapster wallowing about

in ignorance, and the best thing to do with him is to leave him alone. The press keeps him in his exalted position. . . .

Perhaps there was some truth to what Cobbs said about attention, but leaving Robert Shelton alone was another matter. In fact, the pity is that he and his organization were not given enough attention soon enough and taken down long before 1987. Repeatedly delayed justice only contributed extended life to the mindset of the KKK, other cultures of racism, and individuals influenced by them.

By age twenty-four in 1971, I had turned an important corner in racial attitude, and—contrary to Cobbs's admonition—just could not leave the Grand Dragon alone. (Though he became the more nationally influential Imperial Wizard after Cobbs's article, I still thought of him as the Grand Dragon—seemed a better fit.) A graduate school friend and I visited Shelton's Tuscaloosa area home to interview him for a team report we had chosen to do on his declining KKK kingdom. The unpretentious Shelton house was in an upper-middle-class neighborhood. Mrs. Shelton—who set up the interview when I called—greeted us courteously, led us to her husband's office, and asked us to wait. We sat in silence, transfixed by the scene in front of us: on the wall behind a wooden desk, was a large photograph taken at night. Three men stood in white KKK hooded sheets, arms folded on their chests. The figure in the middle was distinguished from the others in some way I cannot remember today, perhaps by an emblem or color of emblem. A burning cross rose behind and above the men. It was an imposing scene. This Grand Dragon had nerve.

Shelton entered, and after smiling briefly and shaking our hands, took a seat behind the desk. Speaking in affable tones, he motioned to the photograph and said something about it being old. It seemed certain that Shelton was the man in the middle. He was not interested in small talk, and asked us to start the interview. If I were interviewing such a person today, I probably would throw him a few softballs initially—but not then. My friend and I had an overabundance of nerve ourselves. We asked three or four questions, and all were dodged or redirected by Shelton. Then, he abruptly said he was running late for an appointment, and he led us out of his office through the front door and onto the porch where he unceremoniously bid us adieu. That interview must have lasted all of five minutes, and only the fiery cross scene and cold shiver it produced in me linger as memorably significant, the average-looking face of Shelton long lost in time. We left the interview dissatisfied, but knowing that Robert Shelton proudly felt the KKK and its bravado was still worthy of display—that photograph being worth the proverbial thousand words.

The following excerpts are from a *New York Times* article that appeared on March 7, 2003, shortly after Robert Shelton's death at the age of seventy-three. It says much about him, the effect of the Donald case, and the gutting of the KKK:

> The verdict in the Donald case coincided with the end of Mr. Shelton's Klan activism, his son said. . . . Mr. Shelton shared the Klan penchant for secrecy. After he lost power, when an all-white jury awarded Mrs. Donald the keys and the title to the United Klan headquarters, he was difficult to reach, living in Northport, Ala., near Tuscaloosa and shunning the activities that had been his forte, his son, Robert, said.
>
> In 1994, he told the Associated Press: "The Klan is my belief, my religion. But it won't work anymore. The Klan is gone. Forever."

The article also reported that Shelton's son and daughter rejected the premises upon which their father based his KKK activities. I can't help but wonder how long he held to the Klan as his *belief* and his *religion*. Once, I considered that the fire-filled image behind Shelton's desk might have been indicative of his still-fervent beliefs, but now—more than ever—I know that's not my call. People do change, and I am no one's judge. However, I do know that this "Dragon" was not, by any stretch, "Grand."

15

Stories That Need Telling

The preface to this book portrayed it as a potential contribution to a new dialogue on race. That objective took root after I had been writing for several years when—as a part-time sociology instructor—I addressed the subject with a racially balanced college night class of working adult men and women in their mid-twenties to forties. Not telling them how to view anything, I shared a short summary of my story after which they were asked to tell and discuss their own race-related experiences in small groups. Floating from group to group, I found discussions to be lively and on point. We reconvened to discuss group reports, and it was apparent to me that many students seemed to derive some benefit beyond academics from the activity, a personal benefit. The same results were evident with two subsequent classes composed of different members. Class evaluation forms and follow-up talks with random members validated my conclusions. They needed this free expression, this new personal dialogue.

I was convinced that something important came from the unencumbered sharing of long-untold personal stories and views about this vital subject. I dove back into my book and rewrote, researched, and wrote anew with enthusiasm and the conviction that my story and those of many others need to be told. In that spirit, this chapter details more of what happened to me after the hot summer of 1965, and ends by introducing chapters that tell some of the stories of people who lived in Greensboro through the turbulent sixties and up to the present. The turning point I reached prior to the interview of Robert Shelton was not a literal point in time at all. It was more the approximate middle of a curve. The curve was not only influenced by people and events already described in this book, but also by thinking away from Greensboro, outside the bubble.

Sometime late in undergraduate school, I developed a vision of becoming an attorney—always defending innocent clients and always winning like Perry Mason in the TV series of the same name. After all, there were the childhood courthouse and courtroom fantasies, and a grandfather and cousin graduated from the University of Alabama School of Law. I completed my undergraduate degree in political science, and my career path seemed to be a straight line. The straight line held up through a first semester of law school, after which I came to the realization that the practice of law would not be like my fantasy, always defending the innocent and always winning. The second semester was a half-hearted experience after which I began looking for a new direction—sans prayer because then I thought nobody was on the answering end of those calls. Wandering into an unknown building near the law school, I started reading bulletin board notices and was drawn to a poster of an Uncle Sam-like man with top hat, clad in red, white, and blue. He was pointing a finger toward me, a la the classic military recruitment poster. However, the caption said, *Social Work Needs You!*

My ruminating on leftist images of bleeding-heart social workers was interrupted by a voice from behind: "Are you interested?" I turned to see a stocky middle-aged white man. Answering his terse question in like manner, I replied "Interested in what?" "Social work," he said. I replied that I was not even sure what that was. He introduced himself as Dr. Charles Prigmore, invited me to his office to talk, and I obliged—having absolutely nothing better to do.

Prigmore quickly learned that I did not want to pursue law, wanted to help people, and was trying to sort it all out. He immediately responded that I could get a full Children's Bureau stipend to complete a masters in social work. His description of the profession included helping people, with alternatives such as counseling, administration, and juvenile justice—all things that did not fit the little old welfare lady image. I said, *Okay, I'm interested.*

My father was in denial about this new direction—tough for him to say his son was in social work. He generally avoided the subject thereafter, still preferring fantasies. It was some time later when I found that he led some people to think I was still in law school or had entered medical school—something else, anything else. Actually, I did not subscribe to many of the more liberal positions often attributed to social work and later found that there were many like me in the field.

While graduate course content in those days was pretty generic, I leaned toward a concentration in community organization. Bringing people together to accomplish things was something I enjoyed, similar to athletics. A good teacher and man, Dr. Jerry Griffin, took me under his wing. In time, I was engaged in practical community work in Tuscaloosa as well as projects like the interview with Robert Shelton—integrating everything with related reports and lecture/discussion classes.

Some hands-on experiences especially challenged my assumptions about black people as well as poverty and prompted a sharper turn of the attitude curve, again not a product of lectures. I needed a summer job after my first year, and stayed in Tuscaloosa to work with an urban renewal project funded by a federal grant. Our job was to help low-income people, predominantly black, who were about to be displaced from their long-term homes. Our concentration was implementing a youth recreation program. There were a good number of teenage boys and young men living in the area, and more than a few bore the sole weight of manhood in their homes. Some were responsibly diligent, and some were in and out of trouble constantly. Others were just overwhelmed.

Knowing my love for sports, Dr. Ray Sumrall, director of the program, asked me if I wanted to join him in forming and playing on a flag football team composed of local black guys and the two of us. He said it could be a little rough, and we would play in some low-income areas at night where we would be the only whites in sight for miles. Young and still believing I was virtually indestructible, I never entertained a negative thought about it.

Some guys on the team reminded me of myself at their ages, rebelling against visible authority and/or some absent father figure. Some with severe attitude problems quit the team, and a few didn't stay due to violating terms of probation or tough situations with their families. Some did not think beyond the end of their noses, confronting things with their own versions of a tire iron, maybe a knife or even a gun at times. I found that some held stereotypical views of me and Sumrall—bubbles being bubbles no matter where they exist. Then, there were the ones who were pretty unselfish and unpretentious despite their circumstances.

At first, a few fights broke out among team members, but nobody was ever seriously hurt. Flag football was an outlet for sure. Playing with those guys helped me understand more about poverty than any instructor could ever have gotten across. It was hard for them to work together, so abundant were their distractions and mistrust. Getting to know players individually and their families and seeing the team coalesce into a unit, I was part of something that transcended race, really for the first time in my life—and possibly for the first time in the their lives as well. Black and white guys grew into supporting each other and working for a common goal. Those with some dreams of heroism or attainment were like me in that way. After a lot of testing, good hearts surfaced. Many were believing Christians, something I initially tolerated and later appreciated. We also played in a city league for fast-pitch softball, and though there was a knifing incident in the crowd once that caused a game to be delayed, spectators were generally courteous at all games. All things considered, people were just people.

On another front, through an assigned placement, I helped a predominantly black group living in a large public housing project organize a residents' association to negotiate over housing conditions and start self-help projects. Many of the residents were senior citizens. All were solid citizens. The association grew, and I was surprised that so many were willing to work for worthy objectives and wanted the best for their community. Faith was a big factor for most of these good people. One black lady in her mid-seventies impressed me with her knack for verbally nailing down conclusions in a succinct way. We became friends, and I learned to seek her advice on challenges in helping the association get organized. She was gentle-hearted but smart, determined, strong-willed, and quite willing to share her views.

As a core of residents and I worked to get others involved, including knocking on doors, I found some living there were not to be trusted. We held the association meetings at night. Once, there was a police raid near our meeting site. Sirens were blaring. When I got up to go to the window, my senior friend grabbed my arm and said, "Honey, you sit back down right now! You just might get shot!" When I sat down, she asked a man in the group to lead us in prayer. It turned out that someone had been knifed in a fight over drugs. It was a no-brainer to see that most of the black residents were brave people with good hearts—no perfection, but again, people were just people.

Another learning experience in terms of culture and service occurred when I accepted Dr. Griffin's offer to help black residents in a subdivision of rundown rental houses deal with a less-than-kind-hearted landlord. If anyone ever lived down to the title of slumlord, he did. Housing conditions were mostly deplorable, without even the most basic services or upkeep. I had never seen so many rats! Not only was the landlord unresponsive, but he was also unpleasant. To him, a resident should be satisfied to have a roof overhead, even if it leaked! When there was a response, he sent workers to do only the minimum possible and rarely in a timely fashion. He could be insulting, even to older women on fixed incomes, who were making rent payments on time and treating property with care.

Little did I know at the beginning of the project that I was the only one taking it on, with the benefit of Dr. Griffin's supervision of course. I got to know residents and—enlisting the help of a local black minister—took on the slumlord directly on more than one occasion. At first, he was insulting to me, and his responses gave me the strong feeling that he regarded me as a white traitor, similar to a scalawag or the way I had regarded white demonstrators not that many years before. His racism was evident in one preliminary talk I had with him before the minister came into the picture. Together, we obtained some begrudging concessions from this man, but I got a lot personally from the struggle.

I will never forget the kindness and humility of the overwhelming number of those people who lived in deplorable conditions and were so mistreated. Faith was a repeating theme, and they found good in the worst circumstances. I never encountered any disrespect from any of them—even when telling them things they did not want to hear. There was only gratitude. People were just people, and good people were indeed good people.

Experiences like these put meat on the bones of my developing view about myself and others. I was moving in a distinctly different direction on the curve and went into the day-to-day working world with a totally different attitude. When I started in the School of Social Work, I knew I wanted to help people. I did not know my experiences serving others would have such a strong effect on how I viewed my attitude the day of the march several years before. I finally knew, in my heart as well as head, that there was no way a person's skin color or socioeconomic status dictated anything about their hearts or heads.

I had known black people like my mother's helper Sarah in Greensboro, but my cultural context and youth did not allow me to get to know more of them better. Also, I did not see the connection between the way I viewed them and my need to feel good about myself relative to them. Now, serving and working side-by-side with black people handling the cards life dealt them, I saw not only their hearts and minds but also my own more clearly. Many of them had stronger hearts. Some were smarter than me in practical ways. Some were definitely wiser about life, and they overcame obstacles I doubt I would have overcome. A fact gained enduring traction: I was in no way *better than them*.

After graduate school, I served in as a mental health caseworker and counselor for about four years. Then, during a hiatus between jobs, I determined to study the Bible on my own to solidify my opposing view to my wife's strong faith. I attempted to find conflicts between the four gospel accounts of the New Testament. Nobody, including my wife, knew I was doing it. The conflicts I found in those gospel accounts turned out to be minor or easily understood in context. Putting it simply, I got to know more about Jesus and his claims in the process, found him to be irrefutable, and this time fiction became reality for me.

A handful of years after becoming a Christian, I took a church campus minister job. My wife and I befriended and helped students of many backgrounds, cultures, and colors for six years until we felt that our young children needed a dad who was not playing basketball on campus at night and living with a figurative revolving door on our home.

Since then, my work on behalf of vulnerable children and families has been ministry without a ministry title, just a Christian. I understand that everyone who cares about people in a genuine and colorblind way is not necessarily a Christian. I've worked with and respected such people who have done good things for others. I'm also thankful for friendships with people who have different perspectives than mine. Again, mine is just one story. For me, living a Christian life has made my service and desire to do what I can about racism more proactive, humble, and effective, with staying power. I may not often see the results, but my faith tells me it makes a difference.

As for my hometown in the Black Belt, its updated racial disposition was an unknown when starting this book. I did not want to form conclusions without seeking first-hand answers to crucial questions. I had changed since 1965 but what about Greensboro? Is it different today for a child growing up there, black or white? What is it like on Main Street now? My feeling was that the best answers to these and other relevant questions should come from people whose lives in Greensboro spanned from those turbulent sixties to the present. I determined to interview four of those people with three objectives:

1. to obtain clarity on some facts and different perceptions about the culture and the traumatic events of summer, 1965;
2. to compare race relations at that time to the present; and
3. to identify potential ways to improve if improvement is still needed.

I set up interviews with two black and two white individuals. The blacks, both women, were both participants in the Greensboro demonstrations. The whites, a man and a woman, were my 1965 Greensboro High senior class-mates, the last segregated class. One white resident and one black resident lived within the city limits at the time of their interviews. The two other white and black interviewees lived in the county nearby, as will be described.

The two black women had lived in the area since the events of 1965 and up to the time of their interviews without interruption. The white man and woman both attended college away and returned to live in Greensboro afterwards and up to their interviews. The two black women are referenced with their married names as they gave them to me. I knew neither of them previously. The first names of the two whites are used because they were my peers in high school. All four interviews far exceeded my expectations.

Early in these interviews, something struck me that demanded more attention than I had previously assumed in regard to racial perspectives. I knew, from my professional and personal experience, that socioeconomic status affected many vital things more than I had thought previously. However, my assumption about racism was that poverty paled in comparison to other contributing factors. Some things emerging from the interviews—involving education, the local economy, and jobs—told me I had underestimated the effect of rural poverty on race relations. Therefore, in order to have an adequately informed backdrop going into the interviews, I'm providing the following brief summary of information and perspectives on the economic history of the area since the Civil War. As always, I claim no expertise—only facts and, hopefully, a little common sense.

MY SEARCH LED ME to the conclusion that the effects of slavery lasted through the civil rights struggles of the mid-twentieth century and even up to today to some degree. When D. F. McCrary established his fortune in the mid-nineteenth century, Greensboro was in Greene County. Hale County, with Greensboro as the county seat, was formed from parts of three counties, mostly Greene, in 1867 after the Civil War, and named for an officer of the Confederacy killed in the war. This is relevant to understanding pre-emancipation statistics listing Greene and not Hale—also subsequent stats referencing each separately.

According to the 1860 census, the first and last with a separate schedule for slaves, Greene County's total population was 30,859 people. That included 23,598 slaves or more than 76 percent of the total. After emancipation, the 1870 census on the new county of Hale showed a white population of 4,832 and a black population of 16,990 or almost 78 percent black. A revealing statistic from that census is that, of 11,871 people age ten and older who could not write, 11,318 were black. Think about what that meant!

A cultural key, in Hale County and much of the Black Belt, is what happened to freed slaves and their descendants after the war. As the post-war economic decline played out, sharecropping began to make up for some lost ground, and cotton made a moderate comeback. Then, enter an insidious insect called the boll weevil and the great cotton crash going into the 1920s. Crop diversification helped, supported by the scientific work of George

Washington Carver, ironically a man born a slave who was hired by Booker T. Washington to head the agriculture department at Tuskegee Institute. Carver introduced several alternative cash crops for farmers (including sweet potatoes, soybeans, and peanuts, for which he also developed hundreds of new uses) and introduced methods of crop rotation that would also improve the soil of areas heavily cultivated in cotton. However, it was not enough. The crash and Great Depression had a big effect on many white Black Belt families including well-to-do ones like mine. Ours was more a matter of fortune lost, but many people, black and white were totally bereft. For the black residents, the isolation of many in this rural area, education levels that were still far behind those of whites, and the lack of job availability, left them with few opportunities for progress.

Primary industries changed over time through the twentieth century in Hale County and some other Black Belt areas—from cotton to cattle to catfish—but with an attendant decreasing number of employees needed for these types of businesses. There is much to be said for the area adaptively holding its own through times of change, but that also means generational poverty would not easily be broken. Going forward in the twenty-first century, even more adaptation will be needed to maintain a subsistent economy. As of the time of this writing, the catfish industry is in a downward spiral, and I'm not sure that any major employer will fill the void. There is still no gold in kudzu.

Hale County's predominantly rural population, according to the 2010 census, was 17,975 people, a decline of 1.6 percent from the 2000 census. The state's total grew by 5.9 percent in that time period. As for white and black populations in Hale County, their shares in 2010 were 41.3 percent and 57.7 percent of the population, respectively.

Hale County's proportionate majority population of black and rural dwellers pales in comparison to its proportionate poverty rates, a pattern shared with most of the Black Belt. The status of children tells the story. According to Kids Count 2010 data for Hale County, about 44 percent of black children were living in poverty, compared with a relatively small 10.5 percent for white children. Also among black newborns,19 percent of their births were to unmarried teenage mothers—compared to just over 5

percent of white newborns. This has a huge effect on the prospects of future
generations, considering practical and emotional implications for children.

Economic and population indicators say the same thing about the Black
Belt and Hale County today. Freedom is a wonderful thing, but most black
people in the Black Belt are free to be poor, and it is not getting better. Some
may leave for opportunity's sake. However, when poverty is entrenched,
people enduring it are often stuck where they live—especially if they live
in a rural area. An August 22, 2004, *Mobile Press Register* article written by
Larry Lee pointed out that there were fifty-nine mayors of all town areas of
the Black Belt, and they represented an average of about 1,500 people each.
Lee stated that "finding a critical mass of such things as leadership, finances,
or trained workforce . . ." in most of the Black Belt is very unlikely. With
about the same number of residents as Greensboro (twenty-five hundred
plus), Moundville is the other relatively populous town in Hale County.
However, in contrast, it is growing. Within easy commuting distance from
Tuscaloosa and with a greatly improved highway connection in recent years,
Moundville is often an exception to the dismal statistics of Hale County.
Without it, a bleak picture would be even bleaker.

This scenario of entrenched poverty has spawned several governor's
commissions and panels; all promising to make a big difference without
delivering significant long-term results. Some people have resorted to promoting development of a new north-south interstate highway through the
area. Others say that such projects will not be fruitful unless there are major
industrial or business commitments first. There are some positive develop-
ments underway today, but the crucial point is that nothing promises to
free this area from its high poverty rates—predominantly rural and black.

In a twist of history, the emancipation of slaves formed a new type of
bondage—sometimes called an albatross—that strapped Southern areas like
the Black Belt with a massive force of unemployed or severely underpaid
people. The patterns have continued, and someone might be tempted to
say it has been a matter of the sins of slave-holding forefathers being visited
on future generations. I understand that proposition, but I believe it more
important to understand that today, most of the real fallout victims of the
sin of slavery are clearly black citizens, not the descendants of slaveholders

or other whites. Another potential conclusion is that poverty only increases the odds against making substantial progress in race relations, a matter deserving attention when considering the level of change in terms of racism and race relations in Greensboro and the Black Belt. This was one of the factors borne out in my interviews with four experienced and perceptive area residents. I found their thoughts to be both informative and moving.

16

Black in Greensboro—
Then and Now

ALICE HARGRESS

On arriving at Mrs. Hargress's home, I did not know what to expect, having only talked with her briefly over the phone. She lives in Cassimore, an unincorporated rural area just south of Greensboro. Her daughter greeted me, and invited me into the living room. In a few minutes, Mrs. Hargress came in and greeted me with an engaging smile. She looked considerably younger than her age—ninety-five at the time of our interview in late 2009—and her nimble approach almost disguised the fact that she used a cane. The sporty hat on her head also belied her age, but the lettering on the front said much: OBAMA.

During the lengthy interview, this elegant lady was thoughtful and quick in response to questions, with an impressive memory. She referenced some of the more fuzzy facts with good-natured chuckles and reminders of her age. She seemed to be a wise and discerning person—happy about the successes of her children and their offspring. Afterwards, I thought how blessed Mrs. Hargress's family has been by her example and guidance for so long. The good do not always die young.

I couldn't resist asking if she wore the Obama hat for my benefit. With a broad smile, she said *sure!* She enjoyed answering the question without need to elaborate, but I continued the pursuit. She expressed her pride in having a black man in the White House, saying that things have come a long way since 1965.

We talked about the demonstrations in Greensboro in the 1960s. Mrs. Hargress and a friend decided to participate when word spread that an important march was about to take place in town. She saw it as an opportunity to do her part in gaining the right to vote but not for her alone. She kept thinking about how her mother had never voted.

"They said we couldn't vote. I said, my momma, my husband, my granddaddy couldn't vote. We had to do something! I was associating with the SCLC (Southern Christian Leadership Conference) through a local committee, meeting here and there. I was secretary, so I went and learned what was going on. I was superintendent of my Sunday school, found out they was marching for the right to vote. I said we ought to."

The tone of her voice and the look in her eyes spoke volumes to me about earnest foot soldiers of the civil rights movement of the fifties and sixties. She drew a direct line between the right to vote and human dignity, not so much her dignity as the dignity of those she loved.

Mrs. Hargress was not one of the "virtually all juveniles" referenced by the *Watchman* article about the marches—she was fifty years old at that time and a leader in her community. She and her friend were late the first demonstration day due to a time mix-up. On returning the next day, they were full participants and recipients of unanticipated consequences.

Though this foot soldier didn't know the exact dates, her description pretty well matched that of Richard Stephenson, the white demonstrator who called himself a "Negro" when police asked him a sarcastic question about his race. Therefore, I concluded that she was relating her account of events on July 28, 1965. I later gathered that accounts varied somewhat depending on exactly where individuals were at a particular time in a sequence of events, on which day or days they participated during three consecutive days of demonstrations, and the groups into which they were separated by local authorities when questioned or arrested. However, these two accounts were unmistakably the same as to a particular day and events following.

Mrs. Hargress said there was a lot of talk by leaders about the earlier church burnings. This reinforced my speculation that a calculated response to those burnings was in play to some extent. It was just before passage of the Voting Rights Act, so a national agenda certainly may have been involved as well.

As Mrs. Hargress spoke with such deep conviction, I thought even more skeptically of the *Watchman's* dismissive description of "largely a bunch of noisy juveniles apparently more interested in silly antics than in anything else." She remembered starting at the St. Matthew Church and knew there were some whites among fellow demonstrators, but she had no specific recollection of Stephenson. She knew the short black woman I saw in the other march and recalled that she was among those in this one. I finally learned her name: Minnie Coats, living in Tuscaloosa at the time of the interview. Miss Coats was one of the older youths who took part; she was a youth leader in her church at the time.

Mrs. Hargress remembered seeing an angry white crowd across Main Street from the barricades at Morse and Main that blocked the marchers and that those white men were all holding a variety of crude weapons. She said a number were white folks who had done whatever it took to *qualify*—to be *deputized.*She added that she was surprised to see that a white neighbor of hers had done that—that she would not have expected him to be involved. I took this to mean she was disappointed.

She continued her story, recalling that "a bomb or something like that" blew up beneath the steps to the minister's house located near the church. Her description led me to think it was the tear gas canisters the *New York Times* reported as being thrown at the church and parsonage where the Days lived. She said that Reverend Days' young daughter was on the porch at the time. This tear gas canister was not the same as the snarling dogs or church bombs in Birmingham, but this still made me think about how children were in jeopardy during those days.

Mrs. Hargress remembered being urged by their leaders to begin marching. Fearful but prayerful, she was determined to follow through with her convictions.

The organizers' original route to a burned church building was to include another courthouse visit, but white authorities intervened, and demonstrators were led to a location near the post office less than a block away on the other side of Main Street from the barricades. Mrs. Hargress remembers seeing buses parked and waiting on the curb. At each bus, in addition to the driver, one man with a gun stood by the front of the steps.

At the bus steps, demonstrators were asked individually where they were going or wanted to go. If they said anything other than "to the courthouse," they were released. If they said they were going to the courthouse or down Main Street to march, they were told something like, "Well, march yourself right on into that bus." Mrs. Hargress told the man that she was going to the courthouse, so she joined the others already on the bus.

Buses loaded with demonstrators were driven fifty or so miles to Selma after leaving Greensboro around 10:30 or 11 a.m. When her bus arrived and was parked in Selma, they were told to stay seated. She thinks the experience to that point was the same for the other few busloads she could see. It took several other buses for the entire group to be transported. There was no air conditioning in the buses sitting there at mid-day during the hottest time of the year, and they were parked in the sweltering sun for a long time. She didn't remember exactly how long they stayed there, but it had to be as many as ten hours and well into the night before they left—from the information she gave later.

From the bus, she could see tags of parked cars around them, many displaying a disheartening and frightening sight: the letters *KKK*. Feeling sure it was done for their benefit, since a number of cars with those tags were all parked there, those onboard the bus agreed to pray to God in humility like children. "We said we got to sho nuff pray now."

Those on her bus knew they were headed to jail, but were surprised to learn that all the jails in the area, including Linden, Thomasville, Marion, and Selma were already filled with their fellow demonstrators. Mrs. Hargress felt that authorities were trying to figure out where to put them, and that's why it took so long. She said their bus and a few others were finally driven toward Uniontown on Highway 80 to what she described as a *roadhouse* to be incarcerated since jails were full. From her description, this was the location where Richard Stephenson was incarcerated that same day, the place he called "Camp Selma." However, she did not remember seeing him or other white men there. It was about 11 p.m. by the time Mrs. Hargress's bus and the other one arrived at the facility, where they were fingerprinted and photographed.

There were no bars, but Mrs. Hargress knew the roadhouse was some type of prison facility because she saw officers moving other prisoners out in order to accommodate them. She recognized one man, a relative who she knew was serving time. There were many more women than men on the buses that arrived at the roadhouse that night. Once prisoners were moved out, police escorted the demonstrators into a building with one room and a partition so that men and women were divided into two spaces. The original area where the women were placed was set up to house only four. It was so crowded that you could barely move without touching someone. A lot of time was spent standing rather than sitting, since sitting caused more contact.

The guards brought in a big open container filled with water and placed it in the center of the women's room. It was the only source for drinking or washing, Mrs. Hargress recalled. It was a "washtub and a little pot with a handle for drinking. Had to drink behind everybody. Say I just now had it in my hands. You just drop it back in. It wouldn't sit on the water. You had to reach down in the water to get it back out. It was miserable."

Bathroom conditions were worse: "People want to go to the bathroom. Here they come and put a potty in the middle, set off from the water—no way to hide. Everybody see everything. All that was really tough."

Then there was the food. "We were fed with thin cornbread and big beans cooked down to gravy. They were real soft, and I couldn't swallow them. The thick liquor is what I could eat. Some ate, and some didn't. We had about five white girls. I really didn't know them."

Later, she said about the white girls, "I would like to meet them now."

The crowded conditions, the food, and not being able to bathe led to a lot of physical distress and a bad stench. Beyond and above the physical agonies, Mrs. Hargress recalled the sheer humiliation and embarrassment.

Her roadhouse stay lasted from late Tuesday night to about noon on Saturday. It was impossible to sleep, but the women kept their spirits up by singing and praying.

In order to leave, a demonstrator had to have someone post bond and arrange transportation home. Her family did not have a car and owned no land as a basis for bond, so she had to rely on others for help. All these years later, it was difficult for Mrs. Hargress to tell this story. Her eyes welling with tears betrayed the pain and embarrassment she still bore. Dignity is priceless. For this refined woman, it was timeless. My face must have betrayed the utter disgust I felt to think about what she endured as a result of her peaceful and unselfish effort to obtain the right to vote.

Despite her ordeal, Mrs. Hargress was positive about the aftermath: "We did accomplish what we went out to do. They did pass it, and my momma was able to vote. My son bought me a car, and I took my mother and my husband's grandfather up there, and we voted."

I asked about race relations in Greensboro today compared to 1965. She said she felt good about changes. If she gets in a line now, white people coming in later must stay behind her. Restrooms are available to all, regardless of color. Today, a black person can walk down the Main Street of Greensboro "any way they want to." There's no space expectation by whites. She said that sometimes whites and blacks talk sociably, more than in the old days. However, she said she doesn't go downtown much anymore. "It has dried up down there."

In discussing why downtown had *dried up*, she first acknowledged that a lot of people just go to places like Tuscaloosa or to Walmart in other locations to shop. Then, she said something revealing. "They didn't know we know it, but folks are grown up." I took this to mean that black adults are not like children who have no insight about what is really going on. She went on to say that local businesses "sold to folks but they went to Tuscaloosa to keep from wearing what we wear. My daughters came here from California. They were walking down the street, saw a dress they liked. They wouldn't sell it to them cause didn't have cash. They went to Demopolis and used cashier's checks or whatever to buy what they wanted there." She seemed to feel that her daughters were not trusted beyond cash in the Greensboro store.

I was not ready to come to any blanket conclusions about fashions or merchants from this account. However, I did think perhaps it illustrated how—by practice or by perception—racial sensitivities may still run high in Greensboro today.

On the positive side, Mrs. Hargress told me about a white man who runs the biggest store in the countryside not far from her. "He treats folks like he trusts them, black as black or white as white. He's a millionaire or could be because folks flock there." She said some white people act like they trust black people today, so it is progress compared to the sixties.

As for hiring practices, she said she thinks business people have a long way to go with race relations. She said if a white boss has two people applying for a job, one white and one black, the boss is more likely to pick the white person. She hastened to say that's not true for all white employers. She also qualified it by saying that "Mexicans" coming in had made the situation worse. I took that to mean any Hispanic person. According to Mrs. Hargress, they are often hired over young black candidates for jobs because employers know they will take lower wages, and blacks will not.

She said the wages are too low, but she did not let black youths off the hook with that. Her greatest concern is for black youths who just give up in the face of such hiring practices or low wages. She said that many get negative attitudes and don't keep trying, or just refuse to work for the wages. Then, they get into "no-good behavior." She was very passionate about this and said they are forgetting how their ancestors were treated. She felt the youths need to appreciate what was sacrificed for them and "remember how folks fought for their rights." They need to take advantage of all opportunities and build up from there, not give up. "They are blessed, and they need to know it."

As for how real change takes place, Mrs. Hargress summed it up in her response to my story of brandishing the tire iron at age eighteen. "You grew up in it. It gets to be your fault if you pass it from your generation to next. It will pass if you let it pass. We can't do anything more than what we see when growing up."

Regarding Perry Smaw's murder, she knew something about an older black man being killed back then but did not recall anything about race being involved.

Mrs. Hargress is still very active in her church, Cassimore AME Zion, serving on the board of trustees. I asked her if she thought area churches could help with race relations.

"We've talked, and think it's two or three white churches today that will allow black people to come without problems," she said. "They will meet you at the door and give you a seat. Others have ways to let you know you're not welcome."

She spoke of a white girl from New York and her friend who were in the area doing research and writing. They attended the Cassimore church regularly, and were welcome. Several whites in the area came to two of her birthday celebrations at the church. She was pleased about that. I asked about predominantly white and black churches getting together at times. She said it was a good idea but didn't know of it happening.

Mrs. Hargress's full name is Alice Sledge Hargress, and her ancestors were slaves who worked for the ancestors of Anne Sledge Bailey, the white woman I was to interview later. She said she and Anne are friends, and she was happy to have Anne attending her birthday celebration and to have been interviewed by her for the local newspaper. Mrs. Hargress's ancestors worked for the Sledge family for a long time, and she said they were proud to have the Sledge name—as is she today.

Driving into town after the interview, I thought about my frustration over not finding the true family names of black people who were enslaved and took on surnames of plantation masters or had their identities only recorded by nicknames. Yet, Mrs. Hargress described two families—black and white—former slaves and slaveholders, maintaining a shared name and mutual respect long after slavery ended. I took it to mean that no two people necessarily see all such matters in the same way. Even more compelling was the fact that this dear lady and her younger white friend, a descendant of the family that once owned Mrs. Hargress's family, could be friends. It fueled my hope, and I looked forward to getting another take on this. Driving through the University of Alabama campus later that night, I mused about a ninety-five-year-old woman teaching a life-and-race-relations class. She would do a great job.

THERESA BURROUGHS

From one brief exchange on the phone to set up the interview, I expected Mrs. Burroughs to be responsive and direct. I was not disappointed. Like Mrs. Hargress, she had been receptive to the proposition of an interview on hearing my purpose, but she was very inquisitive about the specifics of what I had in mind. She was rightly concerned about how her nonprofit organization in Greensboro, the Safe House Museum, was going to be affected by anything published. Having worked as a nonprofit administrator with organizations serving good causes, I could relate. After learning more about the organization, I told her I was hopeful that results would be positive for the Safe House, a historically appropriate site for our interview. Mrs. Burroughs was courteous and informative throughout our interview—straightforward and succinct with perceptive insight.

There was no mistaking the advantages of recall this foot soldier has about civil rights events of 1965. She was very active during all of the Greensboro demonstrations that summer, and participated in others beyond Greensboro. Later, Mrs. Burroughs devoted herself to preserving associated historical artifacts and facts, and her efforts led to establishment of the Safe House Museum. Therefore, she has a uniquely practiced memory about relevant facts.

The Safe House Museum is so named since it was formerly the home owned by Mrs. Burroughs's family where Martin Luther King took sanctuary when being hunted by the KKK. Located at 518 Martin Luther King Drive, the museum offers uniquely informative materials including an interesting video and other vivid portrayals of events and the overall struggle for civil rights.

An excellent example of the scope of the Safe House program was presented in an unexpected manner for both of us. During the interview, a black man dropped in. He owns a farm purchased in the area not long ago. It was at least part of some land that was owned by whites in the nineteenth century—likely, part of a plantation. He said he had found something in an old barn on the property that Mrs. Burroughs might want in the museum.

Unfolding two dirty, off-white cloth items, he asked us what they looked like. I had no idea. He explained that they were white harvesting bags that slaves filled with the cotton they picked. Seeing the way they were designed to be slung over the shoulder, I recalled paintings portraying slaves bent over in the cotton fields picking and loading up those shoulder sacks. I also remembered written portrayals of the physical pain borne by slaves picking and cleaning cotton, especially when unreasonable managers overworked them.

Mrs. Burroughs was delighted with this man's kind offer to contribute these articles to the museum. Frankly, it produced an unexpected and un-identified emotional response in me.

Later, after the interview and on my drive up to Tuscaloosa, I was near tears as I considered slavery and something tangible, something real from the time—something symbolizing so much about slavery in the South. I thought about the bartering of human beings and the separation of families. I thought about the nameless ones who cannot be traced in history and the sheer agony of being confined and owned by others. Whether slaves were treated indecently, or even somewhat decently, did not matter. I was overwhelmed by considering the immensity of the burden of being owned. I was thinking of all those lost dreams, opportunities, and hopes; of the separated families, physical torture, and lost identities—the sheer cruelty of slavery. I tried to relate, but I could not. How long would the pain last, or be repeatedly revived, even when those people with the sacks strapped over their shoulders were long gone from this earth? I was even reminded of the strength and growing faith that the burdens of slavery produced in human hearts. All these lingering thoughts came from seeing that solitary, single item brought in by the farmer.

Mrs. Burroughs led me through many displayed pictures of demonstra-tions and the famous and not-so-famous people involved. As we approached a life-sized mannequin wearing a genuine KKK hooded white outfit, my mind drifted back to Robert Shelton and the photo behind his desk. My thoughts dwelt on the sacrificial freedom struggle that preceded and included those demonstrations, among them the march I witnessed.

Looking at the original wooden floor, I thought of the KKK in hot pursuit of Martin Luther King, and the opening of the Burroughs home to him for sanctuary at their peril—truly a safe house. I had heard that the video there presents an excellent portrayal of what transpired that summer. Limited by time after the interview, I had to return a year later to see the film. It did not disappoint me.

When I referenced Mrs. Hargress, Mrs. Burroughs said, "That's her pic-ture right there." A closer look revealed that Mrs. Hargress looked every bit the distinguished woman I met earlier—forty five years younger, yes—but with the same kind eyes.

Mrs. Burroughs affirmed that the man who actually led Greensboro demonstrations that summer was the minister at St. Matthew, the Reverend A. T. Days, referenced earlier in news accounts and now located with a church in Mobile. He was the Bible-holding minister in the front line of marchers I saw at the courthouse.

I told her that a number of the whites in Greensboro despised the marchers but white demonstrators, such as Richard Stephenson, really made us mad. She didn't remember him specifically, but in recalling her experience over many demonstrations, she said that whites like me viewed the white demonstrators as "nigger lovers. They beat them so bad."

Among whites who helped with voter registration and other civil rights efforts in the area, two young men stood out in her memory. They arrived in a VW Beetle to drop off two others. Mrs. Burroughs said it was the first time she had seen a *Bug*. In the summer of 1964, they came from California, stayed here with local black families for a few nights, and then the two traveled on to Mississippi.

"The rest is history," she said. "The poor things got killed over there. Those two guys." She pointed them out in a photograph. Their names were Andrew Goodman and Michael Schwerner. They and a third young man, James Chaney, were murdered by members of the KKK somewhere near Philadelphia, Mississippi. The shocking news reverberated across the country and was a wake-up call for many people.

I mentioned my memory of a short woman without naming her, and Mrs. Burroughs instantly said, "Minnie! That's her picture." She pointed, and I rose to get a closer look at the photograph on the wall. Ms. Coats looked exactly as I remembered her, and she stared into the camera lens in the same intense way she did with us boys when we taunted her in those days. I said she seemed like a tough person. Mrs. Burroughs affirmed that Ms. Coats was a strong and determined woman but also a kind person, who participated in demonstrations faithfully and remained an active church member over the years.

I related that when Alice Hargress and her friend came to town to demonstrate, they apparently did not expect what they got. Mrs. Burroughs said they were not alone: "You never knew what would happen for sure."

Mrs. Burroughs remembered participating in the march to the courthouse that I witnessed. When I mentioned the singing of "Amazing Grace" before the violence broke out, she said it was a song they sang a lot during demonstrations as they did others, like "This Little Light of Mine." I asked her about news accounts of a verbal exchange between the mayor and someone in the crowd. She said that was not the mayor: it was between Reverend Days and the man over the Water Board who was telling them to disperse. I took it that she felt the mayor was relatively passive, and that this particular city employee was just more assertive at the time.

I mentioned my memory of violence starting at the front of the crowd, and said I was not sure who—the authorities or the rowdy bystanders—first took violent action until viewing news accounts that said it was the latter. She could only confirm that someone with the city had a stick of some type and did strike one demonstrator on the head causing him to bleed severely. She identified the injured demonstrator as Eddie Long.

Mrs. Burroughs showed me a photo of her taken during the demonstration. She was thin and wore a stylish set of large sunglasses that were pointed at the ends. I remarked that the glasses sure made her stand out. She said she was known for those sunglasses. Despite the flamboyant eyewear, her expression in the photograph was serious and determined—not unlike those of others on the walls. I thought not only about the gravity of the issues involved, but also of demonstrators who were under the realistic threat of violence. She said she weighed only a hundred and ten pounds sopping wet at the time. Yet, she was a force for freedom.

Among the photographs was one of former U. S. senator and vice presidential nominee Joe Lieberman who participated in the Greensboro demonstrations, coming in as Stephenson did while still a college student. Other now well-known participants included Marion Barry, later mayor of Washington, D.C. I asked about Jesse Jackson and how she perceived his part. Mrs. Burroughs said he was about the same as today, "into his religion and civil rights." She said he was just out of college, and they invited him to come for the demonstrations. In addition to Reverends Days and Thomas Gilmore (the pastor from Eutaw that Stephenson referenced), she said there was a Reverend Grant who was very active also.

In recounting events associated with days of demonstrations, Mrs. Burroughs did not remember Stephenson's account of a sudden downpour that tamped the gas and energized the crowd, but there was a good reason. "They knocked me out with that gas and had to take me to the hospital. I missed that part." She spent the rest of that day in the hospital. I recalled the *Watchman* article that said some were incapacitated by tear gas, but *most* made it back to the barricades before the rain fell. Again, she didn't recall much about that, which confirmed another variable about the recall of individual demonstrators. It could be a matter of whether or not they were conscious, unconscious, or injured!

Like Ms. Hargress and Stephenson, Mrs. Burroughs was transported by bus to Selma and from there to incarceration at the roadhouse. Their accounts were very similar. I remarked that it was a long time ago, and much must be difficult to remember, but she quickly corrected me.

"No. You remember a lot when you go to jail like that."

Over the years of the civil rights movement, Mrs. Burroughs spent several nights in jail in different places due to participating in demonstrations, including Thomasville, Selma, and Birmingham. This determined woman was not only gassed for her peaceful efforts, but she also had those Birmingham dogs set loose on her. Today, she relates it all in such a matter-of-fact manner. It was just something that had to be done.

Mrs. Hargress had had no specific recollection about the Perry Smaw murder. Now, I asked Mrs. Burroughs if she could remember the name Perry Smaw, and I waited for her reply. She responded, "Is he the one that got killed?" She had no remembrance of it being associated with anything racial. I told her about the news reports that a black man was convicted with the motive being theft, and I said I was assuming that was the sum of it, if nothing more surfaced from research and interviews.

In regard to my personal racism and the culture around me in those days, Mrs. Burroughs said that she felt that I held up the tire iron against blacks in general, not against an individual. She said that a lot of times, it's like that—meaning people assume blanket views without consideration to individuals.

Along these lines, in regard to Sarah, my mother's helper, she said, "She would have given her life for you." It was consistent with my view of Sarah and individuals like her with good hearts—key word: individuals. Mrs. Burroughs's words on culture and families reinforcing racism were also succinct, clear, and to the point: "It was put in you from your momma's kneecaps. Changing? It's like going against your religion—takes a generation."

When I asked how things had changed, Mrs. Burroughs responded enthusiastically. While agreeing with Mrs. Hargress that young people need to remember more about what was sacrificed and not give up on employment and other things, she said it's her belief that the good thing about the young people, black and white, is that "They don't hate as fast and as hard and deep as in those days"—at least, not regarding race.

Her view is that an important aspect of the imperfect efforts at school integration is that some white and black youths are able to play football, baseball, and basketball together. They play as a unit, she said, and that bonds them. She also described some positives from her daughter's experience being in high school with white youths. She was secretary of the senior class, and a white male youth was president. The two young people got to know each other one-to-one, and they became good friends—key term: one-to-one. It wasn't that way between blacks and whites before except for some blacks who worked in the homes of whites—some practically becoming family. We talked about not having opportunities to know each other through the theater, school, and churches. Then, we talked again about Sarah.

Mrs. Burroughs told me about a letter she received in recent years from a white man who was young when the demonstrations occurred in 1965. "He was like you. He had this black woman who would come and help clean up. He forced his mother to fire her because she was demonstrating. Over all these years, it was still bothering him. He couldn't rest. He saw the Safe House, just flipping through the internet. He wrote me this letter, and said he wanted to apologize to her. She still lives here in town. I got them together, and they met each other. He apologized."

Another story involved a white man she read about in a book. This was not a local story. His son married a black woman, and they had a baby, a girl. He disapproved and kept his distance from the little girl as she grew to be a toddler, but he was at a family picnic when a dog started growling at his granddaughter and started to run toward her. She then ran up to him, crying "Granddaddy, Granddaddy!" and jumped in his lap. He put his arms around her. Mrs. Burroughs smiled and said that he was "hooked from that day forward."

Mrs. Burroughs's final story concerned her visit to the doctor just a few weeks ago and how change occurs through day-to-day life. A white woman's baby boy started crying in the waiting room just as the doctor called his mother in for her appointment. To help the young mother, Mrs. Burroughs picked up the crying child and saw that he had a funny look on his face. She said, "Um, hum, you haven't seen a black face before, have you? But in this world, you are gonna see a lot of us."

The mother left her little son in the waiting room with Mrs. Burroughs. By the time she came out, her little boy was "just squealing and laughing," having a great time with Mrs. Burroughs. The mother was amazed and thankful and expressed her appreciation to Mrs. Burroughs.

I think this founder of the Safe House, a daring woman who participated in demonstrations and suffered due to it, saw this interaction with the little boy and his mother as a "brick-laying experience," as she would talk more about later. She believes that living right in relating to others day to day is at least as important as participating in demonstrations.

Later research led me to an online recording presented by StoryCorps. It featured Mrs. Burroughs telling her daughter a story about her efforts to become a registered voter in Greensboro. Only two minutes long, this video presented a fascinating example of what she encountered trying to register over a period of years; how she was subject to harsh, demeaning treatment. It also captured the determination and persistence of foot soldiers like her, and the pivotal role played by ministers active in the civil rights movement but receiving little credit in the course of history.

When I posed that it seems churches could do a lot now that has not been done to help race relations, Mrs. Burroughs agreed. She sees downtown as different today, noting that white people treat blacks differently.

"The whole atmosphere is different." However, she did not mean it was all good. She agreed that it was a good thing that blacks can walk any way they please, but noted that some black youths will "knock you down." But of course, she noted that Greensboro is in need of revitalization and few people are now downtown when it used to be busy. "The streets are just bare."

In regard to continuing racial tension, she believes it is still there. However, it is changing and will continue to change: "And then people talk about why don't you do this and that? You know, we've just been free for forty years. We were in slavery for four hundred years. How can we eradicate all that in forty years? Generations unborn has to do that. It will be done a brick at a time."

Her words really made me think. It has now been close to fifty years since the freedom marches occurred, but it's such a short time in the course of history. Also, it struck me that Mrs. Burroughs is right in another way: Real freedom is more proportionate to equality than to freedom from literal slavery. Gaining the right to vote was crucial to obtaining that freedom from another form of slavery. In her thinking, so much of what remains is a matter of laying those bricks, one at a time.

Before I left, my host asked me to help her fasten a large, informative poster to the wall. It portrayed a timeline for events in the history of the civil rights movement. I was having a difficult time getting thumbtacks to go into the hard wall, which she found as yet another opportunity to educate. "Slaves put this house up," she said, "You know they did good work."

Driving toward Tuscaloosa as the sun descended, I thought about the symbol of the harvester's shoulder bag, Mrs. Burroughs's sheer grit and bravery, the KKK's pursuit of Martin Luther King, the meaning of freedom and forgiveness, the relatively short time black people have experienced freedom, and brick laying. A beautiful sunset and some sleep at my sister's home helped calm a racing mind, but only until the next day's interviews when the marathon for understanding was on again.

17

WHITE IN GREENSBORO— THEN AND NOW

RONNY CRAWFORD

Ronny Crawford and I were casual friends in high school. In my research I learned that he also witnessed the courthouse demonstration in 1965. We never discussed civil rights events when we were classmates, and we really hadn't spoken at all since then, except for a few brief summer encounters. On the phone, Ronny gladly agreed to host me at his home. I was surprised to learn that it was located on the corner of Main and Otts streets.

As soon as I parked, Ronny came out to greet me with hospitality and enthusiasm that lasted throughout the interview. Before we entered his home, I inquired about a magnolia tree that once occupied the middle of Otts street with a single street entrance lane on one side of the tree and an exit lane on the other. It was gone, but I could make out the dirt area in the middle of a grassy median where the massive tree trunk had been rooted into the ground.

He said that his son used to enjoy perching on its massive branches, but added that the old tree rotted and was unearthed several years ago. I told him the spreading magnolia was a site of fantasy and real refuge for me at fearful times—then told him about a day when I was in hot water with my intoxicated father for some unremembered offense. I related how—from one of its massive branches—I could see over the top of a few houses downhill to my back door where he stood calling my name, slapping the doubled belt on his hand.

Ronny's parents raised chickens commercially in 1965; they had an office in town, about a block off Main Street. He was working at his parents' office the day of the march, and they told him not to go to Main Street that day because they heard there might be trouble. But when someone told him the march was taking place, he couldn't resist taking the short walk to see what was happening.

Ronny came to Main Street in time to hear and experience only the end and aftermath. "I was standing in front of the dress shop. Elmore's was across the street, and I was standing on the corner," he recalled. "I don't remember seeing them assembled, but remember hearing them chanting and singing around the courthouse. They were already there. Soon, I saw them bolting. I remember later knowing there was something about the permit."

He assumed they were going back toward St. Matthew, and they were in a hurry—a "stampede" he called it. One fleeing black youth ran into him or hit him with a forearm on the back of his head. He wasn't sure about the way he was bumped or hit, but it knocked Ronny's sunglasses off onto the pavement. "Of course, I was reaching down to get them, and when I looked up, here comes another guy, and he squared off with me. He just looked at me, and I looked at him. He ran on. No blows were exchanged. I just remember black men running, mostly young."

When told my experience, about the tire tool becoming dead weight in my hands, he said, "You were rejecting the idea to use violence subconsciously."

At some point in later demonstrations, Ronny drove by the blockade at the intersection of Main and the street where St. Matthew was located. He was not sure when, but he saw the demonstrators massed behind the blockade. This was sometime during the same three days of demonstrations ending in the thwarted march and busing to incarceration at Camp Selma—as described by the two previous interviewees and Stephenson.

Ronny recalled that he heard later about the demonstrators being bused to Selma to be put in jail. He was told a number were taken to what he referenced as an Alabama Highway Department facility on Highway 80. He knew that they were "crammed into the building with no facilities or anything."

Ronny, who worked with the State for some time, insisted there are still buildings on that site and labeled as Alabama Highway Department facilities—not necessarily the same buildings as in the sixties. He gave a detailed description that seemed to conflict with what Mrs. Hargress told me about prisoners already being in the building she was to occupy. Later, it dawned on me that Highway Department facilities made sense if those prisoners were members of what we then called a *chain gang* or were working for the State in some capacity as was often the case for prisoners in Alabama at that time. When we traveled back then, we frequently saw prisoners, wearing black-and-white-striped uniforms, working on the side of the road. They worked for the Highway Department, but were supervised by officers.

Like me, my former classmate recalled nothing about Perry Smaw's murder—more reinforcement for certainty on that matter. When I broached the subject of race relations in Greensboro, he reflected on all the things I remembered about the cultural discriminations in place growing up.

Unlike me, Ronny said that he never went downtown much then and does even less now. He said in those days there was never any fear about being in the minority compared to blacks on Saturday streets, but such a lack of fear was the case generally. "We slept with doors open, right? There were more blacks here then than ever, but we were not afraid." He was right. We had no fear of the black people back then. Though Ronny did not say it, I assume there is some fear now.

I asked Ronny if he remembered any pranks particularly directed at blacks when we were kids or teenagers. Without hesitation, he told me about how he and some others went out in a car and bombed the top of tin-roofed houses with Coke bottles. He was surprised to learn I had the same memory. Though neither of us could remember the other's involvement, we both recalled two of our friends who participated.

He thought we didn't recall each other because there was probably more than one of those bottle-bombing trips. I winced at the thought, and told him I had felt bad about what those families must have experienced. Ronny agreed that they had to be terrified, and agreed that as white boys, we had no reason to fear being caught or what local authorities would do to us if they had. He also agreed that we would never have thought of doing something like that to white families, poor or otherwise. Ronny was pretty certain that nothing like that ever happens in Greensboro today.

Due to their chicken business, Ronny's family employed a labor force of black people. "It was a rotten job to care for chickens. It stinks, and it's hot," he said, adding that wages were extremely low, and only those desperate enough would do the work. For two dollars earned, they often owed his dad one. They would charge lunch purchases at a local store to him, and he would take it out of their payroll. I told him my dad, as manager of the local poultry plant after serving as a deputy, deducted what was owed him from payroll as well, but that was more of a loan payment collection, not lunch reimbursement.

Unlike my memories, Ronny couldn't recall that his family emphasized superiority over blacks; he told me about a black girl they called *Puddin*. He said she was older than the children in his family, might have been ten at the time, and was the daughter of a black woman who worked for them. Puddin was put in charge of some five-year-olds in his family. Speaking of an incident involving her, he said, "A cousin or somebody said *nigger*, and grandmother told him 'Don't you say that about her or anyone. They can't help it if they are colored.' I think that type thing softened or blunted the effect of all that."

I asked, "You did call them niggers, didn't you?" He said he did, but never to their faces and never before his grandparents. He said Mrs. Burroughs's father once told him that his grandfather was a good man who never cursed blacks or yelled at them with disdain.

Ronny could not recall any Greensboro teachers reinforcing racism, and also considered Miss Mary Martin a very positive influence regarding the value of humanity—with never an ill word about anyone, racially or otherwise.

He surprised me with his clear memories of the day President Kennedy was killed. He called it "the crucial year for us when John Kennedy was killed." He remembered that one of our classmates left for lunch and came back joyfully saying that Kennedy was killed. He remembered that Principal Key called an assembly after everyone was buzzing in celebration about it in the halls. According to my former classmate's recollection, Key "had everyone wanting to crawl under their seats because they were expressing joy over it."

As for the girl who brought the news, Ronny said, "Before the assembly was over, she was squalling like a baby." Ronny and I agreed that our perspective then was that Kennedy was trying to give blacks everything and take it away from us. We had been told that blacks were going to take over our school soon, and we were very upset with the Washington crowd and Kennedy. It did not help that Kennedy was Catholic and from Massachusetts. Ronny added that, in rebuking us, our principal said people all over America were crying on TV.

In Ronny's opinion, Key's stern response generated considerable trauma and was a crucial turning point for us in forming our views on race relations, whether we understood it then or not. I thought my classmate was probably right, and I probably underestimated the effect. We needed to be confronted forthrightly by someone we respected, something everyone needs at times, especially when it comes to wrong attitudes about important things. Ronny said Key told us something we had not heard in our upbringing or in our community: We were wrong! He compared the few days following Kennedy's death to the destruction of the Twin Towers, remembering that most public events were suspended—with the exception of Auburn and Alabama football games. He said he went to an Auburn home game, and the announcer had everyone stand for a moment of silence.

Consideration of our high school and its role expanded as we talked about how our class was the last to be segregated. We had a top-notch school, a source of pride that was important and that we saw as threatened in those days. Ronny said graduating from that school was almost a religious matter for many. "I remember the bitterness of the families; that half of them said, I'm keeping my school I supported with my taxes. Little did they know their taxes wouldn't keep more than one teacher, even the way they're paid here. In my opinion, those most distraught were the ones from north Hale." He had more depth of insight about this than I had. Later, I found out why that was true.

I thought back to Alabama's historical resentment in the 1830s over Federals running people off formerly Indian-owned land they felt they had rightly claimed; the Civil War and abuses felt through Sherman's march; post-war carpetbaggers and harsh outside controls; the subsequent *albatross* of slavery-induced poverty. Reinforced culturally, resentment was not a matter of the distant past to whites, any more than it was to blacks, when the civil rights movement began to flourish. I thought of Mrs. Burroughs's statement that real change takes generations.

Ronny went on to say that, once integration took place, black students were not racing to our formerly all-white school. In his opinion, schools remained de facto segregated for over forty years. While some black students attended our formerly segregated school, many students might be bused to one school for something specific and then back. The football team conducted its activities at the formerly white school, renamed Greensboro West, while the basketball team was at the formerly all-black school, Greensboro East. I later found that Ronny's token integration contention was supported by media coverage, including a 2003 article pertaining to Greensboro in the *Mobile Register* (today called the *Press-Register*), titled "Parents May Sue to Integrate Schools." Unlike Mrs. Burrough's individual bricks view of change, Ronny's concern was more systemic and culturally broad.

As for poverty, it is Ronny's contention that those most distraught historically were actually whites in north Hale County. In Alabama's early history, they did not get the best land taken from Native Americans and cheaply ceded—the black loamy soil south of Greensboro. Instead, they got the less productive land to the north. The prime fertile land south of Greensboro, then called the canebrake, was ceded for a dollar an acre. The cane that gave the area its name was easily burned off to make room for cotton, and the cost of slave purchases could be made up from cotton revenues within a year. Cotton made white kings in the south canebrake while white poverty grew in that less-productive terrain to the north. This then, Ronny concluded, was one of the primary areas for deepening white poverty during the Depression.

He proceeded to share with me his theory, developed from a race relations course and considering Hale County's rampant poverty. He agreed this historical perspective could be applied across the Black Belt area according to two distinct groups: the have and have-not white populations before and after the Civil War. Losing their slave labor and power, no matter how wealthy plantation owners had been, they were in the minority. They couldn't do much politically except stir up the passions and resentments of those mostly poor whites who lived there in greater numbers.

In Ronny's view, many of the large land owners wanted "to force them to see they were oppressed by an outside force." As that agenda succeeded, the poor oppressed whites became the oppressors of blacks. It made poor whites feel better to consider themselves better than the blacks, but both groups remained oppressed by poverty. The only way to get out of it was through education. Poor whites in north Hale County went to some elementary school near them, and when they entered the seventh grade, they could attend at Greensboro and finish high school there. Disadvantaged and oppressed, many were held back a year and never finished. Completing an education at our school could be the key to getting out of poverty. In the 1960s, the poor whites in Hale County perceived the efforts to raise the quality of education and equality for blacks as a threat to that way out. They took that threat very seriously.

Ronny's great-grandfather's name, James Francis Crawford, is also inscribed on the statue in the center of the courtyard in Greensboro. Unlike my family's fortune based in the lucrative canebrake, his family's gains came by way of that less-than-prime land to the north and their own devices. I have my story from the rich plantation base to the south, and Ronny has his from embattled poverty north of Greensboro. Both stories should be appreciated for how they have interrelated and affected race relations in the area. This also helped me to understand Ronny's greater appreciation for the educational opportunities present at our high school, something I took for granted.

My host took a book from the shelf to show me photographs of the faces of white poverty in central Alabama—much in north Hale County. It was an epic chronicle by James Agee, first published in 1941, *Let Us Now Praise Famous Men*. He implored me to look into the eyes of the people, especially those of impoverished children, saying it compared to photographs from Bosnia. "What do you see in those eyes? Where is the hope? There's nothing there!"

In my professional career, I had looked into many eyes of distress and poverty. What I saw on the pages of that book was extreme.

While acknowledging progress, Ronny still believes that racial animosity cuts both ways among some in Greensboro because they continue to blame failures on someone else. He said the town's economy has gone downhill: "Just drive through." He also said "I think there's more animosity of blacks toward whites and hence, whites have become antagonistic to some extent in that the failures of themselves are still being blamed on the blacks. If it wasn't for them, the blacks' and schools' problems . . ." He felt that this pertained more to the "boomer generation" people than anyone else.

Ronny said if tensions have not been over education problems and the strange way integration was handled, it has been over the depressed area economy. What has happened to Greensboro has happened to many small towns all across our country, but the Black Belt has not yet been able to get much going business-wise that can bring adequate employment opportunities for generational rural and poverty-stricken people.

When asked about the role of churches, my former classmate was opinionated, saying it was and still is "the most segregated hour in the USA, not just in the South." Today, he attends what he called a relatively liberal church where if blacks come, so what? There are only a few of those in the area, as Mrs. Hargress also said. Back during the civil rights era, he remembered that men guarded the church door against any such possibility.

Ronny referenced involvement with a national effort, *Teach for America*, saying ninety teachers were coming down to seven Black Belt counties from eastern schools. They will get stipends and will integrate with faculty to assist in tutoring students with such needs. He said the effort started in Mississippi where they "raised test scores in the Delta by a phenomenal amount." I replied that this sounds like a worthwhile anti-poverty project, but—with entrenched poverty and lack of work opportunities—a question is how many students with those increased test scores will remain or return to develop new business in the Black Belt. Ronny said there is nothing to bring them back and agreed there is no gold in kudzu.

We discussed various Black Belt initiatives from governors and legislators and talked about the push to get an interstate route through the area. Ronny pointed out that "some of the poorest counties in the US are on an interstate."

As an example of good race relations, he recalled a recent trip to a Tuscaloosa store where young blacks and whites seemed to work together well and enjoy each other's company. Such relationships may exist in Greensboro businesses, but he really couldn't say because like most others, he doesn't shop there much if at all.

I drove away from the interview thinking that Ronny's forum and those of others would be contained in this book—not that I would lobby anyone to necessarily adopt Ronny's perspective or opinion on how things came to this point or future potentials. I do believe that much understanding and perhaps even untapped energy for good, rests in the intersections of our stories and opinions, and his are very intriguing. Also, I was struck with the increasing theme of poverty, the struggling local economy, lack of jobs, and human tendency to blame problems on others. It had become obvious to me that these factors have affected and continue to affect race relations and inhibit growth of relationships. Later, driving through downtown and taking the time to notice as Ronny said, I was struck by the number of vacant storefronts.

ANNE SLEDGE BAILEY

Anne Sledge Bailey was also a member of my 1965 graduating class. Like Ronny, she went to college and returned to her hometown, as a teacher in her case. Then, she became co-owner and manager of a downtown hardware store with her husband. Anne has written pieces for the *Greensboro Watchman* about Greensboro's history, architecture, and residents. Other than email exchanges over recent years in the role she assumed to help our class stay in touch, my post-graduation contact with her was scant. We never discussed civil rights activities or race relations until I enlisted her help prior to interviews, but she became an invaluable local resource.

I was pleased to find that Anne's thinking on racism and associated events of the past had recently been stimulated by her own activities and related associations. She was an enthusiastic interviewee with obvious concern for the people of the Black Belt. The Baileys reside just south of Newbern, an even smaller town located nine miles south of Greensboro. At the time, they commuted into Greensboro to run their hardware business. Anne grew up in Greensboro proper, but her parents did not allow her to be anywhere near those 1965 summer demonstrations.

A black woman, Lula, worked in her family's household and participated as a marcher. After the marches, she never came back to work at Anne's home. Some time later, Anne contacted her. She visited with Lula for years until her death, but never asked her about the demonstrations or why she did not return to work at her home. She did not know for sure that her father fired Lula, but said ,"Had Lula come back, I seriously doubt we would have talked with her about it."

Anne recalled some things Mrs. Hargress told her about participating in the demonstration and being imprisoned. She thought what they went through was horrible and that "stepping out and being part of the civil rights movement must have been scary." Recently, a black man told her that a white man in town had guaranteed him groceries during any boycott at the time, provided he did not participate in demonstrations. He said that he did not participate in them as a result.

Shielded by her parents, Anne did not know much that happened with demonstrations until years later when Theresa Burroughs educated her. This was yet another affirmation of Mrs. Burroughs's efforts and the value of the Safe House Museum. When I asked if she remembered the short woman who participated in demonstrations, she quickly identified Minnie Coats because she knew her over the years since. Anne had taught her son and said Ms. Coats was a wonderful person.

Anne told me that Ms. Coats served on the city council before moving to Tuscaloosa, and said she did not mind taking positions contrary to those of other members, black or white. She remembered one occasion when Ms. Coats did not stand with other black members regarding an especially hot issue. It appears that she was not one to be restrained by any bubble for long. Why was I not surprised?

As to Perry Smaw's murder, Anne also remembered nothing about it. Combined with follow-up news articles, feedback from these four interviews just solidified my conclusion that justice was indeed served by convicting someone whose motive for Smaw's murder was theft: case closed, without a doubt, for me at last!

Anne also did not know anything at the time about the church burnings. Like me, she admitted to not being very informed and being pretty self-centered at that age. She also recalled nothing about the KKK rally at the football field but did remember and identify with Ronny's description of our earlier shaming in the school assembly after the death of President Kennedy. She said "It did challenge me to consider things, to think."

Anne said she and her sister were not even allowed downtown on Saturday much at all even though they lived in close proximity. Her attorney father's reasoning was clear: "If a black person ever said anything improper or came across sexually to us, he said he would want to kill him. We were not allowed to wear shorts downtown, to shop or do anything downtown."

I told her I was down there a lot. She reminded me that I was not a girl, and I worked in the downtown area. Sometimes I'm amazed that I have to be reminded of such things, as with Ronny's reminder of leaving our doors unlocked.

Anne admitted that racism was all we knew growing up but insisted that her parents never berated black people, and treated them with some degree of respect. Her father may have been gruff with them, but she said he was like that with everyone. However, she said blacks never came to the front door. They tooted their car horns to let her family know they were there. She was taught not to politely say "Ma'am" to black females regardless of age. White people considered black adult females to be *women* while white females were considered *ladies*.

Anne said the racism in people still comes up, and will likely take generations to change completely—if it does at all. She has seen it in some of her family members, drinking at a party and talking with loose lips. "Out comes the 'nigger' jokes, and who says anything? Nobody! Nobody!" I asked if she thinks we need to be calling out people like that. She said she was writing positive things about her black friends, and hopes her writing reflects her attitudes racially.

I asked her about walking down Main Street today, thinking I finally had someone who still walks down there. Anne's words seemed to portray that race problems cut two ways. She said many young blacks seem angry. If she speaks to them, they do not speak back. She added that she would probably be angry too if she was as poor as many of them. I thought about Mrs. Hargress's concerns about black youth and Mrs. Burroughs's statement about blacks having their genuine freedom for a relatively short time.

As a former educator in the area with a sister who teaches mostly poor black students in Mississippi, Anne's thoughts on education were well-considered. She said increasing overall education levels will take more than short-term projects. Many getting good educations will leave. Those with college educations who return, black or white, are not guaranteed good money. She said there's some hope that the recent purchase of a sprawling state-owned cattle ranch (previously housing working prisoners) by the conservation organization Forever Wild might help by bringing in tourists and other outdoor enthusiasts.

She was not enthusiastic about the future. "I've got four college degrees and don't make a decent living. Right now, I think I will never be able to retire. Nobody can afford to live in the rental house I have. We had a catfish pond we rented but no more. We have a farmer with dairy cows around our house, but he's in bad shape on money due to the dairy business."

I considered that Anne is a person who those in poverty probably consider well-off and would hope could offer them jobs. Her statements to the contrary say a lot about the historical inability to generate opportunity that is consistent across much of the Black Belt.

Anne mentioned how corrupt government officials affect hope and racism in Alabama generally. She spoke of how some high-profile black officials found guilty of graft, one in Birmingham being an example, have been so quick to project racial persecution. She felt that such things affect many people's racial views both ways, white and black.

My former classmate expressed concern for those in poverty, and she sees they are under-educated. "For every one pulled up, there are hundreds who don't have any opportunities. A big problem here is out-of-wedlock babies." It shocked her when a doctor described his horror of having a mother come in with a fifteen-year-old daughter, thrilled to find she's pregnant out of marriage and without any commitment from the baby's father. I thought of the discouraging statistics on this in the Black Belt.

Anne agreed with the perspective that distressed people look for someone to blame, and race is a convenient place to put that blame. Educational conflicts do not help. She said that, for a long time, there was an agreed percentage applied to black and whites enrolled in Greensboro East and West schools. She feels it was a wise thing to do, but the proposed high levels of integration were never reached and the percentage requirement was lifted resulting in a merger of the two schools. The facts of the situation were reported in a *Tuscaloosa News* article on May 3, 2009: "School to Merge Campuses in Fall."

According to Anne, as a result of all this, most whites found ways to get their children into either private schools or public schools in other areas, and whites are now in the minority at the school where we graduated. Integration may not have worked as well as desired, but her view is that there was at least some healthy integration before, and now that is threatened. This brought me back to what Mrs. Burroughs had said about associating together in the school environment and her daughter's example.

In discussing how people cast personal insecurities into their racial perspectives, we discussed our family backgrounds and agreed that most of us in our senior class did not know each other's families below the surface. She remarked that she knew of some of my family's struggles, but not very much. Anne told me about her own family, and added that in recent times, she had learned how family dysfunction was more pervasive among our classmates than she ever knew before.

We agreed that back then our families did not talk about problems, and we had few outlets. We talked about the extensive effect of alcoholism among many families, and how our predecessors did not gain much insight due to keeping the lid on so tight. While poverty and a dying town may add fire to racial resentments, unresolved family struggles add fuel to the fire as people seek something of value relative to others. Putting others down may make us feel better short term, but such relative elevation has no lasting strength in our lives. In time, it only leads to bitterness.

Talking about the slave balcony at the Greensboro Presbyterian Church,

Anne said there had also been a separate seating provision for slaves at the Newbern Presbyterian Church. A few years after graduating, she heard church leaders there discussing how to keep blacks out. After school integration, the possibility of them seeking church entrance was definitely viewed as a threat.

It was difficult for her to imagine integration happening at the Methodist church her family attended in Newbern in the 1960s, especially when her father knew the bishop who made determinations about placement of ministers. According to Anne, "He made sure a minister sent there would not be someone who would welcome blacks into church." It was considered a sizable and well-endowed congregation at that time and a plum position for a minister. In recent years, she said one minister did welcome some blacks into the church. He did not stay long after that. I thought of Ronny's statement about the most segregated hour.

Anne said that discussions among church leaders, like she described in the sixties, resulted in plans to escort visiting black people out. While that's not going to happen today, her opinion is that there's not a lot of difference in many churches as far as attitudes toward congregational integration is concerned. On the flip side, she told me about a minister at the Methodist Church in Greensboro who met a black man bringing his son to services. After services, the minister told him that he and his son were an answer to prayer, "so some people are different," she concluded.

Anne's perspective on churches comes from experience. Due to her writing projects and personal interest, she had visited sixty-four churches in the area and had written about some. From her observations, only five could be even remotely viewed as integrated, and all of these were predominantly white in attendance with very few blacks or mixed-race individuals attending. There were a few people of mixed race at a Mennonite congregation, a few blacks in a Mormon group, and maybe a few more than that in the Jehovah's Witness group. There was also an integrated assembly at the local Church of Christ, but the entire group consisted of one black person and four whites. The fifth church, an interdenominational group, was only included because they have periodic joint church singings when a black congregation participates. That's a noble activity, but I don't think it qualifies as to integration. All are relatively small church groups.

We talked about the nature of each congregation she identified as having some degree of integration. They are pretty distinctive in nature. Anyone moving in who was already a member of that particular denomination or group—a Mennonite, Mormon, or Jehovah's Witness particularly—was not likely to choose another group in the Greensboro area because choices are nonexistent or limited at best. All things considered, the groups she named are more likely than others to have at least some integration, obviously not much at any rate.

Anne's experience and knowledge included some all-black congregations. The old argument is that blacks want their own churches and whites want theirs: that's just the way it is. There is some truth in that just as there is in the power of status quo. I thought about the black members in the late nineteenth century who left Greensboro Presbyterian to form their own congregation. Not that I blame them at all, but it does show that there are moments of opportunity for racial harmony in churches if seen as such by any who really want to make a difference. While I don't know what happened afterwards, the white minister who greeted the black man and his son as an answer to prayer is an excellent example of preparation meeting opportunity along these lines.

I asked Anne what could be done about churches and worshipping together, noting that Ronny called it, *the most segregated hour.* "We'll do it as we can," she said, "but if we alienate all those people in churches, it won't help."

In regard to black and white congregations doing things together, she said there is one local ministerial association that promotes joint assemblies at Thanksgiving and Easter. A black congregation felt comfortable enough to join, and there was a joint service in the Newbern church. Not many whites attended, but she and some from Greensboro did attend. That is a start.

I thought about how a little give and take would go a long way toward helping predominantly white and predominantly black congregations to get together. Those good folks attending just might tell each other a few stories. As Mrs. Burroughs said, change happens one brick at a time. As you go, you just lay one down every now and then.

During our visit, Anne expressed her deep respect and appreciation for

Mrs. Hargress as a friend. She was proud that they share the Sledge name. Anne said she had enjoyed being at the Cassimore AME Zion Church with Mrs. Hargress. This interview certainly confirmed what Mrs. Hargress said about their friendship.

Anne summed up a lot by telling me a story: "How can people justify racism? Jesus never told us to judge people by color of their skin. There was a black couple who lived in the cottage we leased to them behind us. The woman wanted to go to church with me. I made excuses. Finally, I said I would not feel comfortable taking her to the church. I said, 'You would not feel welcome.' She said, 'Ma'am, why do you go?' I think about it over and over."

I left without any doubts as to Anne's heartfelt concern about racism and the dilemma she felt about doing something about it. During the homeward drive this time, I thought of the role of churches in making a positive difference. I also considered a team-teaching approach in that envisioned college class on life-and-race-relations. It would be conducted by a couple of friends sharing a name and with family histories intertwined—whose relationship alone carries some solid lessons. All Mrs. Hargress and Anne would need to do is tell their stories together, talk with each other, and allow plenty of class question/answer and discussion time. Sign me up!

18

Better Than Them—Me and My Hometown, a Beginning

It is a long drive from Greensboro to Mobile. On the little two-lane road, I passed catfish farms, Faunsdale, and into and out of Thomaston. On previous drives, Thomaston had seemed to be a pretty barren place, but I always thought my hometown was different. I had been confident I would find some positive comparison of 1965 Main Street to Main Street today, but my trip this time and the interviews challenged my whole perspective. I had driven through Greensboro many times over the years, but could not or would not see just how much it had changed in terms of vibrancy.

In my early research about my hometown and the Black Belt, I presumed little connection between racism and poverty. Examining my own experience and the culture around me, it did not seem that economic status was particularly important to prevailing white perspectives on race. A black person was subject to racism primarily due to historical factors maintained and reinforced by powerful processes of socialization. Other factors played a role to varying degrees for different people. In time, I came to the conclusion that the socio-psychological factor involving self-esteem relative to others assumed a more important role than I thought, definitely for me and maybe for others as well. By the time the interviews were completed, economic status also seemed more important than earlier assumed.

There can be no doubt that economic factors for slaveholders were at work during the pre-Civil War years, and that a large free black population after emancipation, primarily rural and uneducated, met with few job opportunities. Subsequent economic droughts made bad matters worse in regard to poverty among the mostly uneducated rural population, black and white. Reinforcement for racism came through post-Reconstruction white law-making and local rules limiting such opportunity generators as education and suffrage or the right to vote.

Psychologically today, while some people may still be trying—wittingly or not—to boost self-esteem or ego by putting others down, it seems there is also a strong potential factor involving the human tendency to blame someone else for one's problems. In high poverty areas like the Black Belt, race is so evident and so convenient as that whipping boy—whites blaming blacks for many ills and vice-versa. Also, the correlation between poverty, education, and crime is sometimes misinterpreted as a correlation between race and crime, particularly when there is a whipping-boy history involved as it is in the Black Belt.

Attitudes about race are not as they were in 1965—no stark revelation there. Ronny and Anne are prime examples of the white form of that change. However, there are reinforcements that continue to keep racial tensions alive and inhibit the community's growth: the poverty and lack of opportunity, the static religious and educational institutions, the closed dysfunctional families without constructive outlets, the breakdown of traditional family units, and the narrow or nonexistent communication on race relations and poverty. It seems obvious that people must come together to constructively deal with these factors, but that is easier said than done.

The four people I interviewed all see continuing challenges and much room for growth in how black and white people relate to each other and work together for the common good. Progress is encouraging, but a crucial and seemingly unanswered question for those four experienced people is how the long-term process of change will be continued among younger people. While people like Coach Key are still needed to speak hard truths, there is an undeniable need for day-to-day bricklayers, those daring to change their part of history still in the making—to deny traditional restraints, share their stories, and listen patiently to those of others.

One obvious continuing sore spot for my hometown is what has happened and still is happening with public schools and the integration issue. Having graduated with the last segregated class at our high school in 1965, I view the conflicts over education as particularly ironic. My experience with poverty, education, and racial differences has told me that poverty—not race—is a key factor in schools with problems that parents fear.

Raising educational levels of those born in poverty is a worthy pursuit, but the effect is obviously stunted by the pattern of educated people leaving the area, not to return. This is true of young blacks emerging from poverty, but it is also true of not-so-impoverished whites. Some of my classmates are still in the area, but most of us left. Either way, it is a loss of potential innovators and job creators. As one of my classmates from 1965 posed in an email exchange circulating among all of us, "What if we had stayed?"

While much of what I learned while researching this book has been negative, I have also seen elements of hope. Some good projects have made commitments to the area. Rural Studio, within the School of Architecture at Auburn University, has injected practical help through its creative student design and construction projects. The Hale Empowerment and Revitalization Organization (HERO) is a noble nonprofit citizen effort to end poverty through housing, job training, youth programs, and mobilization of resources. In partnership with HERO, Pie Lab in downtown Greensboro is tackling poverty and race relations by promoting community development and job training centered on its own food products and an informal atmosphere conducive to dialogue. HERO's other partners include Habitat for Humanity, Americorps, Project M, and the Ultimate Black Belt Test.

Taking advantage of the plentiful hunting and other outdoor activities, efforts have been generated to attract national interest such as Alabama Black Belt Adventures and the aforementioned Forever Wild. Promotion of tourism in the beautiful rolling green hills and plains of Alabama has promise—even including antebellum historical preservation efforts by private sources. On the northern fringe of Hale County, the University of Alabama's long-term commitment to preservation of and public exposure to the archeological treasures associated with the ancient Native American mounds of Moundville is a proven investment. Some new industries, such as a Hyundai manufacturing plant, have developed on the fringes of the Black Belt. Institutions of higher learning do a lot to bring out cultural treasures, historical and present; the University of West Alabama, the University of Alabama, and Auburn University all contribute to this.

While these are all worthy and needed projects, it is evident that they alone will not defeat both poverty and racism—not like bricklayers recruiting bricklayers. Rural economic development and healthy race relations deserve attention by individual citizens who are committed to finding ways to promote progress. Certainly, as the Pie Lab and other projects promote the bricklaying of constructive dialogue and relationships, they contribute to that end. Still, individuals in the area must participate and even create their own initiatives. Also, people like me who leave must return or at least do some bricklaying from afar through their realms of influence.

From what I have learned, a great prospect for more prosperity and harmony in my hometown is the uniting of two seemingly disparate historical preservation efforts—one involving a treasured antebellum history (represented by historic homes such as Magnolia Hall) and the other a treasured part in the civil rights movement (represented by the Safe House Museum and other historic sites). A good faith effort along these lines could attract great interest from many people in Alabama and beyond. Obviously, churches should play an integral role in this or any other effort toward harmony. It may be high time for spiritual priorities and humble faith to transcend racial and socioeconomic differences—or do more generations have to pass?

As for me, the family inheritance is indeed on its head. It amazes me that I can still get back into the mind of that eighteen-year-old boy on the curb—tire iron raised purely due to the color of someone's skin. Going there has been a grueling process but beneficial in unanticipated ways. My story is just one, but it matters because I am a bricklayer. I have changed, and the iron I raised in hatred toward people of a different skin color is gone. My indifference toward God is gone as well; I'm no longer blind, no longer a slave to fears and illusory treasures. My life, hopefully, has and will serve for the betterment of humanity, not according to skin color—until I reach the only home of true and lasting equality.

My story is also about how people make a difference just by their daily examples: a moment of generosity, a word of encouragement, service rendered without regard to race. It is also bricklaying. It is not about seeing immediate results for the good deeds you do for others or your service to them, but believing that the results will be there. Quoting Max Lucado from his book, *Fearless*, it is about knowing that "It will all work out in the end. If it hasn't worked out, it is not the end."

Racism is the assumption that one race is superior to another. It is an assumption of unauthorized and unjustifiable judgment of others. It is buying my blind grandmother's whisper and all the social and institutional reinforcements to that whisper. Freedom from racism, for a racist, means wrestling with its realities as they apply to one lifetime. It means being a learner and assuming very little.

Bringing my own resolution forward to the present, it would be disingenuous to say that the old whisper never haunts me. However, I now know it for what it is, and I can put it into proper perspective. I am confident that I and my hometown have just begun to progress: Ronny, Anne, Mrs. Hargress, Mrs. Burroughs, myself, and others are still laying bricks. We need to tell our stories—our histories—to others and especially to our children and grandchildren who need to tell theirs to their children.

As a Christian today, a large basis for what I'm continuing to learn about myself and others in this life comes through the telling and hearing of those stories and from two imperatives in the Bible; whispers certainly more mysterious and challenging than the one my blind grandmother passed on to me, "You are better than them." While not limited to racism, the first effectively addresses any inclination toward a racist view of others, and the second effectively addresses doing something about racism. As Mrs. Hargress said, "You grew up in it. It gets to be your fault if you pass it from your generation to next. It will pass if you let it pass."

     . . . *in humility consider others better than yourselves.* — Philippians 2:3
     . . . *Love your neighbor as yourself.* — Mark 12:31

About the Author

With degrees from the University of Alabama, S. McEachin "Mac" Otts was a counselor and director of three private child welfare agencies plus a state membership association of such agencies. He received governors' appointments for several terms on the board of the Alabama Department of Child Abuse and Neglect Prevention and the State Children's Policy Council. Today, in addition to writing, Mac is a part-time consultant. He and his wife, Carol, live in Mobile.

CPSIA information can be obtained
at www.ICGtesting.com
Printed in the USA
FFOW02n0450190116
20390FF